REIMAGINE CUSTOMER SUCCESS

DEAR KRISTIN,

THANK YOU FOR SUPPORTING MY GOAL OF WRITING THIS BOOK. HOPE YOU ENJOY READING IT.

— SASI

REIMAGINE CUSTOMER SUCCESS

DESIGNING ORGANIZATIONS AROUND CUSTOMER VALUE

SASI YAJAMANYAM

NEW DEGREE PRESS

REIMAGINE CUSTOMER SUCCESS

Designing Organizations Around Customer Value

ISBN 978-1-63730-436-5 *Paperback*

978-1-63730-529-4 *Kindle Ebook*

978-1-63730-530-0 *Ebook*

To my boys, who inspire me to keep learning.

CONTENTS

PART 1:

WHY DO WE NEED A NEW MODEL FOR CUSTOMER SUCCESS?

INTRODUCTION:

WHY DO WE NEED TO REIMAGINE CUSTOMER SUCCESS?

Industrial age—Quality management. Automation age—Process reengineering. Digital age—??

Every major economic era gave rise to new management disciplines—a collection of practices, processes, and systems adopted by organizations to support the era's technological innovations.

In the Industrial age, organizations focused on manufacturing products of consistent quality. The focus in the Automation age was on the efficiency of business processes, or how work gets done, and resulted in process reengineering practices, like Six Sigma. The focus of the Digital age is the consumer (yes, that's all of us) of digital technologies, as the innovations impact every walk of life. A more specific focus is on the relationship between the consumer of technologies and the companies that provide these products and services. Customer success can be the new management discipline, a new way to organize and run companies, for the Digital age if we approach it the right way.

In the Digital age, or as the World Economic Forum calls it, the Fourth Industrial Revolution, technologies like mobile and artificial intelligence are changing our very way of life. This idea was put forward by the World Economic Forum in a piece on their website titled, "The Fourth Industrial Revolution: What It Means, How to Respond." These changes are deeply felt in our everyday lives as consumer technology has changed how we buy goods, how we pay for them, how we get places, and how and where we consume information, to name a few. Similar developments enabled by digital technologies are changing how businesses operate. For most of this book, I will refer to customers in the business-to-business (B2B) context, where technology vendors are interacting with other companies.

Just as digital transformation became a boardroom topic at many organizations, customer success became a board-level topic at technology vendors. In the Digital age, the relationship between customers and technology vendors has evolved from being centered around transactions to becoming a more long-term partnership focused on customer outcomes.

In response, Customer Success has evolved into a category in its own right, just like Sales, Marketing, and Product Management. Customer Success has become a category of jobs, a category of software products, and a practice at many consulting companies. There are nearly a hundred software vendors in the Customer Success category per Capterra, a website used to research software in different categories. Customer Success is also a very popular career path for many in the technology industry.

As Customer Success grew into a function, many organizations and leaders realized that success of the customer takes more than just one function. Most companies claim customer success to be a core value and a top strategic priority, but their actions often don't reflect their words. Why is that?

The leaders at these organizations lack the right frameworks to embed customer success in all functions. Instead, we default to doing what we know how to do well—that is building, managing, and improving functions, the silos within the organizations. Customer Success has become one such silo, and significant effort, which is sometimes justified, is spent on building this newer silo. This is particularly true within business-to-business technology companies.

Unlike Sales, Marketing, and other functions, customer success is an outcome and a function. To date, too much focus has gone into building the function without a clear pathway to the outcome. In fact, focusing on Customer Success as a function alone will not help us realize the potential for it to be the management discipline for the Digital age. In short, what got us here will not get us where we need to be.

Let me be clear. There are many challenges to setting up the function of Customer Success, which we will see in chapter two. My intent for this book is not to provide solutions to "here and now" challenges. My goal is to look ahead a few years and paint a vision of what customer success could be as a management discipline.

We need to reimagine customer success as a discipline that informs how we build organizations centered around a common understanding of the customer and success by everyone in the organization. My own experience has shaped my interest and ideas presented in the book.

I have spent the last ten years of my career in Customer Success, working in various roles. I set up a Customer Success function at CEB, a research and advisory company since acquired by Gartner, for our very first software as a service (SaaS) product. I have worked in professional services, implementing ServiceNow products, and have set up scalable programs to arm customer success teams with knowledge and skills to implement ServiceNow best practices. In these last ten years, I saw how different teams were working together to deliver customer success.

Coincidentally, around the same time I joined ServiceNow, John Donahoe, now the CEO of Nike, joined ServiceNow as the CEO. One of the big strategic moves he made was to make customer success a CEO-level priority. All customer-facing teams, except marketing, reported to one senior leader. After three years, the Customer Success function has continued to evolve with a lot of starts and stops and a lot of changes.

I realized that defining a model for customer success is a challenging problem that a lot of smart people at a lot of companies are working on. I wanted to do my share by investigating, learning, and sharing what the next generation of customer success should look like.

I present my point of view divided into three parts of the book: first, we need to review the current state of customer success and its challenges; second, we must develop principles for the new organizational capabilities; third, I will discuss how this model impacts the audience of this book.

Let us start with a definition of customer success.

WHAT IS CUSTOMER SUCCESS?

Before we go too far into the discussion, we should settle on some definitions in this area.

The Customer Success Association offers an academic definition: "Customer Success is a long-term, scientifically engineered, and professionally directed business strategy for maximizing customer and company sustainably proven profitability."

This definition does a good job of setting the right aspiration, and many other definitions out there tend to talk about Customer Success in a similar vein. In addition, there is a smorgasbord of terms—such as customer experience, customer-centricity, "customer in the middle," "customer-first"—that all highlight the significance of customers. We could go on and on about terms used and what they mean. I do not see a point in debating definitions and differences, and I won't spend much of this book on definitions.

To arrive at a good, working definition, I look to an unusual source: someone who can think clearly and whose thinking is not clouded by the complexity of "too much learning," my then six-year-old son. He asked me what I did at work back when I was building a Customer Success team. After several minutes of my explaining my job, he says to me, "So, you help other people do their jobs." That was a moment of clarity.

I borrow a word that most kids understand to define customer success: promise. Customer success is about making and keeping promises to our customers.

CURRENT VIEW/STATE OF THE WORLD

In B2B context, the switch to the software as a service (SaaS) business model has forced a change in the vendor-customer relationship. The SaaS business model has grown exponentially in the last decade. According to data published by Statista, the SaaS market size grew more than ten times to over $150 billion between 2010 and 2020.

In a subscription-based model, customers are not committed to long-term contracts, as was the case in earlier days. Customer success and retention are the lifeblood of SaaS companies, and companies needed to build a new muscle, which is essential to the survival of the company. A common term used in the SaaS industry is "churn," which is a measure of revenue lost from existing customers when they do not renew their contracts.

The beginnings of customer success, as a means to reduce churn, can be traced back to 2004–2005 when executives at companies like Siebel and Salesforce realized that there was no one accountable for customer retention, a familiar story across many other companies. They realized the need for specialized resources and personnel who help customers after the sale is made. They noticed that, without this focus, customers would just stop using their products and not continue to pay.

As more and more companies realized the importance of customer retention, they started investing in dedicated functions to manage customer relationships after the initial sale. These companies concluded that their existing customers were also their most profitable. After all, happy, successful customers tend to spend more.

Customer Success (CS) has become mainstream at SaaS companies in the last ten years, and during this time, it has evolved from an obscure function to being the core part of the growth strategy. As Customer Success made its way from a footnote to the headlines of company strategy, we needed a good definition of what Customer Success is, who is responsible for it, and how we achieve customer success.

A lot has been written about the scope of this new function, where it should sit within an organization, whether customers should pay for the services of this function, the compensation structure, and more. As the function became a staple at many organizations, many new players entered the market offering software to manage the function and consulting services to make the function better.

Yet the general state of CS today is a mixed bag of excitement—a feeling that "we have arrived," confusion as CS tries to find a footing in the org chart, and complexity in defining the scope of this new function.

It reminds of a scene from the movie *Office Space*—a classic, in my opinion—which came out in 1999 and was directed by Mike Judge. In this scene, two "workforce consultants," both called Bob, are interviewing different employees about their roles and what they do. When it comes to Tom, who is a go-between for customers and engineers, the Bobs start with their standard question: "What would you say you do here?"

Once Tom starts explaining that he takes specifications from customers to engineers, the Bobs go into a series of questions along the lines of, "Why can't the customers do that themselves?" and "Do you physically take the specifications to the engineers?" Eventually, Tom gets frustrated and says, "I told you, I deal with the goddamn customers so engineers don't have to deal with them! I've got people skills. I am good with dealing with people. Can't you understand that?" Tom gets fired because no one really understands what he does, and how, if at all, it was valuable.

I can hear many a CS professional's frustrations in answering that question, "What would you say you do here?" Thankfully, the state of the CS function is not going the way of Tom's job in that movie. There is general acknowledgement that customer retention requires dedicated resources and investment.

Let us look at it another way. Imagine asking different parts of the organization, like Sales, Marketing, Training, etc., for a simple answer to the question, "What do you do?" Marketing's answer—"I generate leads." Sales—"I close deals." Training—"I train our customers." Product—"I build new features." It is not as easy to answer that question for Customer Success.

In my view, the problem is not just that Customer Success is misunderstood or poorly defined but also that what we have done so far is not enough. We have spent the last decade on defining the tasks, tools, and processes for a new function. In other words, we have focused on the transactions. It is time to move away from this inward perspective and look at a cross-functional, enterprise-wide model.

There are other business model changes underway that will force this change. Many technology companies are moving to usage-based pricing (instead of yearly 'fixed' subscription costs) or product-led growth models (we will talk more about these models in early chapters). We need to rethink the role of different functions in these new models.

WHAT IS NEEDED?

I believe the next generation of customer success starts by going back to the basics. At the risk of sounding too simplistic, we need to disassemble and understand "customer" and "success" separately and put them back together. If we can clearly identify who our customers are and understand their motivations for buying our product, we will be able to define a more holistic approach to customer success.

Customer Success should not be viewed as a function but rather a management discipline that drives the operations for the whole company. Customer success should be the principle that informs the go-to-market approach for the company—from brand and marketing, to sales, to product development.

It is easier said than done. Surely, if there was a simple solution, we would have implemented it. How can we put the "customer-centric" philosophy, or "putting customer at the center," into action?

Today, it is not uncommon for c-suite leaders, from the CEO to Sales and Marketing leaders, to make customer success a priority. Customer Success leaders often have the proverbial seat at the leadership table, which shows the intent of these leaders. The challenge is in translating intent into action.

It will take reimagining customer success as a means to keep promises made to customers. When viewed with the "promises" lens, customer success becomes a company-wide problem to solve. Customer success is not a onetime event, nor is it a set of transactions that can be managed by one function.

Customer success starts when a prospective customer becomes aware of the brand and continues through the lifecycle of the customer-company relationship. The next generation of customer success will force us to think across silos and consider our priorities differently, starting with a common understanding of customers and the value we deliver.

We should think of customer success not just as a post-sale function, but as a collection of services that different teams deliver to the customer. This portfolio will evolve with the company and its products, and the customers they serve. We cannot stop there. We need to clearly define what it means to instill the customer success philosophy across the organization. What changes are needed in functions like Sales, Marketing, and Product Management?

Lastly, customer success of the future, in the B2B category, will rely on customer data to deliver a consumer-like experience—not dissimilar from our experience as consumers of technology. Delivering customer success will be less about a series of transactions between two parties and more about a partnership to fulfill promises.

WHO SHOULD READ THIS BOOK?

Focus on customers and their success is common at many organizations. Most of these are in the business-to-consumer area, the most famous of which is Amazon, known for its customer-obsessed culture.

My book is meant as a guide to leaders in the business-to-business (B2B) SaaS companies. That is the area where I feel I can offer insights and fill in the gaps. Some of the concepts I discuss in the book can be applied to other companies, but my perspective is skewed toward B2B technology companies.

Anyone who is interested in designing organizations that truly put customers at the center will find this book useful.

They will learn specific tactics they can employ across the customer lifecycle to deliver customer success.

Leaders of early-stage companies can use this book to create a customer-centric operating model from the ground up. Established companies with a Customer Success function can recalibrate their approaches and break down the barriers between silos. All companies will be able to imagine a future operating model where customer success feels like a partnership fueled by the next generation of digital capabilities.

Customer Success professionals—which I use as a broad umbrella for all roles in post-sale functions, such as professional services and support—will find insights into designing a more holistic post-sale experience. They will learn how to custom design this experience to suit their own organizational contexts. They will also learn how to work with other functions and define how they can work better together.

Leaders across Sales, Marketing, and Product teams will see their roles in customer success and the changes they need to make in how they run their teams. They will learn how to change incentives and metrics to truly work across functions.

My goal with this book is to show how the next generation of customer success involves teams across organizational silos coming together. I plan to provide practical guidance to leaders from different functions on changes they can make to work toward customer success. My aspiration for this book is to inspire leaders to reimagine customer success as a new way of doing business and designing organizations in the Digital age.

CHAPTER 1

HOW DID WE GET HERE?

Writing a book on the topic, I felt obligated to find the definition of customer success. A quick Google search revealed many different definitions. A lot of these definitions are published by software vendors, like Gainsight, or professional associations dedicated to Customer Success, like The Customer Success Association. The gist of these definitions boils down to this: customer success is about growing the business by helping your customers achieve their outcomes.

The same sources that offer definitions introduce customer success as a "new trend" or the "next big thing." But is it? Isn't helping customers be successful a principle as old as business itself? The definitions do not offer the additional context of what's new about making customers successful.

In 2002, I was working in an Internal Audit department, which is essentially a services business. The leadership of the department wanted to understand how much time we were spending on different types of projects. I was part of the team that implemented a time-tracking software for my department. That was my first experience with a software vendor-customer relationship.

Thinking about the definition of customer success, I bet the time-keeping software vendor we selected wanted us to succeed, and I bet they knew that making us successful was the key to their growth and success. What is new about customer success today is the role technology plays in our lives, in society, and in the world economy. The breadth and pace of change driven by technology are changing not just our lives but forcing companies—both providers and consumers of technology—to reexamine how they operate. Technology providers have a new responsibility in their relationship with consumers of technology. In this chapter, we will look at customer success in the context of the broader changes of our times with a focus on the business-to-business context.

THE FOURTH INDUSTRIAL REVOLUTION—DIGITAL AGE

Most of us have heard the famous phrase, "Software is eating the world," by Silicon Valley icon, Marc Andreessen. In a 2011 post titled "Why Software Is Eating the World," he writes, "My own theory is that we are in the middle of a dramatic and broad technological and economic shift in which software companies are poised to take over large swathes of the economy."

The World Economic Forum called this transformation the Fourth Industrial Revolution in an article titled "The Fourth Industrial Revolution: What It Means, How to Respond" on their website. In a piece published on their site, they state, "The First Industrial Revolution used water and steam power to mechanize production. The Second used electric power to create mass production. The Third used electronics and information technology to automate production."

In the World Economic Forum's view, the Fourth Industrial Revolution is unlike the other three in its scope and speed of change. In that article, the author says that the changes propelled by the technologies of this era are impacting all industries and all countries and will "herald the transformation of entire systems of production, management, and governance."

In the same article by the World Economic Forum, the author writes, "On the whole, there are four main effects that the Fourth Industrial Revolution has on business—on customer expectations, on product enhancement, on collaborative innovation, and on organizational forms. Whether consumers or businesses, customers are increasingly at the epicenter of the economy, which is all about improving how customers are served."

As business leaders across different industries read this piece, they probably underline and highlight the last phrase: "improving how customers are served." The changes are happening not just in consumers' lives but also in companies that create products and services. This trend was exacerbated by the COVID-19 pandemic, where the pace of changes enabled by technology increased manyfold. The global pandemic is just one instance of external factors that drive these changes. Changing regulations, geopolitical factors, and economic cycles are some other examples that disrupt the status quo.

The business side of technology, B2B category, has been slow to pick up on this trend, particularly the one about "organizational forms." The pandemic has forced all businesses, especially those that offer technology solutions, to rethink how they engage their customers and what they are doing to improve these customers' lives. We must use this opportunity to rethink organizational forms and norms.

Technology-driven transformation—the buzz phrase is "digital transformation"—is thriving in all nooks and corners of organizations, not just the flashy front end. Every single part of any organization, including Human Resources, Finance, Sales, Marketing, and of course, IT, is undergoing transformation.

Technology's role in the transformation, and in some ways survival, of any organization means that the vendor-customer relationship is no longer transactional. Companies are not looking for just software vendors but partners and advisors on the transformation journey—partners, not just in technology but also in their success.

Software companies that step up to this new role and deliver against this new set of expectations are rewarded with loyalty and higher spending on company products and services.

HOW SOFTWARE IS BOUGHT AND INSTALLED HAS CHANGED

Thinking back to the time when I led the implementation of a time-tracking software, I recall the two major steps. First was finding the right software vendor that met all our requirements, like how many of us will use the software, how do we want to set up time codes, what reports do we need for our managers, etc. I felt qualified to do that; after all, I knew how our department worked, and I had easy access to people in my department who would use this software.

The second step was more challenging. I would have to jump through the internal IT department hoops to install the software. I needed to understand what type of server we needed and how much storage would be needed. I then had to learn if there were there any special requirements for this software to run on our servers.

If I had to do the same project today, the second step is almost non-existent. I could go online, find the right software, maybe try it for free, swipe the credit card, and *voilà!* I am done. The last part, I understand, may not be as simple; but the point is that it is a lot easier for anyone to purchase software.

The growth of "as-a-service" business models, based on cloud computing, has made it easy to buy software by removing the friction points in the process. Business leaders no longer need IT to purchase and use software because they do not need to buy and manage technology infrastructure. They can use their own budgets to find technology solutions to solve their needs. When I worked at CEB, a research and advisory company since acquired by Gartner, our research found that by 2014 business leaders were spending forty cents on technology for every dollar spent by corporate IT departments. In other words, IT departments are not the sole buyers of technology, and I suspect that today technology spending is even more distributed across IT and other functions.

While the demand side of technology was changing, so was the supply side. The software as a service market is growing exponentially. According to data published by Statista, the SaaS market size grew more than ten times to over $150 billion between 2010 and 2020. Not only is it easy to buy new software, but there are also that many more options to choose from.

This supply and demand dynamic means customers do not need to commit to long-term contracts and can easily switch to different vendors. Of course, depending on the type of applications, it might take more effort in some cases to switch vendors. The point is that switching vendors is generally only getting easier.

Customer retention had become the lifeblood of SaaS companies, and they needed to build a new muscle to survive and grow. This was the big revelation in the early stages of the subscription economy.

CUSTOMER SUCCESS GOES MAINSTREAM

The Customer Success Association's website provides an informative article titled "The History of Customer Success - Part I" which explains how the Customer Success function evolved. The beginnings of the Customer Success function as we know it today can be traced back to 2004–2005 when executives at companies like Siebel and Salesforce realized that there was no one accountable for customer retention—a familiar story across many other companies.

In a blog post titled "Why Do Most SaaS Companies Fail?" Lighter Capital explains that customer churn—the standard term used in SaaS business models to define loss of revenue from existing customers when they stop paying for the product—is one of the top drivers of failure right alongside poor market fit and ineffective management teams. "You can't sell your way through churn" is well-accepted wisdom in the SaaS industry.

As companies realized the importance of customer retention, they started investing in dedicated functions to manage customers after the initial sale. These companies realized that their existing customers were also their most profitable. After all, happy, successful customers tend to spend more. It became clear that customer success was not just a defensive strategy that manages churn; it was the key driver of growth. For example, according to a 2018 article published in Forbes titled "10 Insights from Salesforce's 2018 Investor Day," 73 percent of Salesforce revenue came from existing customers.

Salesforce, a pioneer in cloud-based product offering, had an innovative approach to supporting their customers. As the company was growing by leaps and bounds, this growth was being built on a shaky foundation. An article titled "The 1 word that saved Salesforce From Certain Doom" on the Inc. website presents insight into Salesforce's early struggles. By 2005, they were losing about 8 percent of their customers per month. "Churn was killing Salesforce, and understanding this one word was imperative to the company's survival.

Keeping customers needed to become just as important as finding new ones." They recognized that much of their growth would come from existing customers and set up a Customer Success program, which is a significant part of the organization even to this day.

In 2010, Maria Martinez joined Salesforce as the Chief Growth Officer, to lead this organization, aptly named Customers for Life. In a YouTube video titled "Customer Success: The Strategic, Financial and Organizational Journey," Martinez says that one of their customers told her, "Marc Benioff was our first Customer Success Manager [CSM]." Benioff is the founder and CEO of Salesforce. This shows Customer Success was a top priority early on in their journey.

ForEntrepreneurs, a website dedicated to helping start-up companies and entrepreneurs, has done some interesting analysis to show the impact of churn using a technique called "cohort analysis." They treat the customers who sign up in a given month as a cohort and track what happens to the overall revenue in two scenarios. In their example, each new customer starts by paying six thousand dollars a month. They published their findings in an article titled "SaaS Metrics 2.0 – a Guide to Measuring and Improving What Matters" on their website.

- Scenario A: The company loses 3 percent of this amount (six thousand dollars) every subsequent month, and at the end of forty months, the company's revenue is $140,000.
- Scenario B: The company gains 3 percent of the original amount (six thousand dollars) every month from existing

customers, and at the end of forty months, the revenue will be $450,000.

The conclusion of this analysis is a well-accepted fact: it is hard to grow the business when you are "leaking" the customer base. It is hard to fill up a leaky bucket. Early customer success efforts stopped here and became "churn reduction" operations. There is more to customer success; it is about attracting the right customers, keeping the profitable customers, and building an enduring partnership from which both parties benefit.

The moral of the story is that revenue from existing customers is the deciding factor for the growth of a SaaS company.

WHAT DOES THIS ALL MEAN?

It is important to look at customer success in the context of technological changes that are impacting every aspect of our lives and businesses. When viewed in this context, it will become clear that to achieve customer success, we need to think beyond the functional boundaries. To decide what the next generation of customer success looks like, we need to start with a deeper understanding of where we are today. That is what we cover in the next chapter.

CHAPTER 2

STATE OF CUSTOMER SUCCESS

"I have had eight to ten managers in seven years," UVL Narayana told me when I interviewed him. He was talking about his initial days as a Customer Success leader at Splunk, a company that helps other companies manage large amounts of data. This statement aptly captures how software companies struggle to define what the Customer Success function is and how to structure it. I interviewed Narayana for this book as he is currently setting up a Customer Success function at a startup called Cribl.

Constant reorganizations and changes to their charters are common for many Customer Success teams—not just at startups but also in more established companies. Is this sort of "identity crisis" natural for a relatively new function? After all, there is no such confusion about other functions, like Sales, Marketing, or Product. Or is there more at work here?

Talking to many CS leaders, it is clear there is a lot of confusion on the role of CS, its placement in the organization, the value we expect to deliver, tools and processes needed, the right mix of skills, and performance measures. The tricky part of clarifying many of these topics is that the "right answer" changes with the company and the product.

CUSTOMER SUCCESS—HOW IT STARTS

"When I started in customer success, it was not even called customer success" is a common sentiment many customer success professionals and I have said at one point or another. Many of these professionals come from technology or consulting backgrounds, having worked in technical roles in software companies or customer-facing roles in consulting companies.

Many companies claim to be born in the cloud, or "cloud native," to emphasize that their products were always offered on the cloud. Customer Success is the first born in the cloud function at many of these companies. As the customer relationship moved from transactional to relationship-based, many of these companies established Customer Success functions.

When Narayana joined Splunk in 2013, the company was twenty times smaller than it is today. Many companies in that stage are focused on growth and acquiring new customers, which helps them land some marquee customers. Everyone celebrates—fist pumps, high fives, and all—the validation of their products. Then, reality hits! Companies implementing products hit road bumps, which is not uncommon for sophisticated products in complex, large organizations.

As a first customer-facing team member for the software product at CEB, it was my responsibility to help the customers implement our product. By the time I joined in 2011, CEB had a successful track record of innovation and growth using the subscription model. We knew what the customers needed to get value from our research products, and our internal processes were fine-tuned to grow a subscription research business. However, we did not know exactly what it took to run a software business and whether similar processes would work.

Over the course of five years, I built a global customer success team and developed processes to support the growth of the product. We realized the model that worked for CEB's other products—which were best practice research studies, data, and tools—did not exactly work for a software product. We needed to be more prescriptive with our customers on how to get value from the product, which was not limited to product training or collecting the right data.

When I started at ServiceNow in 2017, our post-sale customer engagement was focused on product implementations. Coincidentally, John Donahoe joined as the new CEO of ServiceNow that same year, and to learn what was working and what was not, he talked to over four hundred customers. Based on what Donahoe learned, we started talking about customer success as an imperative for the company and have been on a journey where the function has continued to evolve to this day.

CUSTOMER SUCCESS—WHAT IS IT?

Today there is general agreement that customer success is essential for the survival and growth of SaaS companies, but that's where the agreement and clarity on this topic stop. There are many questions, each with many more answers, on the topic of customer success.

One of the questions is foundational: What is the definition of customer success? Even though customer success is mainstream in the industry, there are many discussions around its definition. Is it a function? Is it the outcome? Where does customer experience fit in? In an article on their website titled "The Essential Guide to Customer Experience," Gainsight, a customer success software company, presents an equation: customer success is the sum of customer experience and customer outcomes.

There is another school of thought that places customer experience as the overarching umbrella of all customer interactions. Jeanne Bliss is a former Chief Customer Officer, an author of several books on customer-driven growth, and according to her LinkedIn page, fondly known as "godmother" of customer experience. In one of her books, *Chief Customer Officer 2.0*, she outlines a five competency framework that is a guide for leaders to organize enterprise-wide activities to earn "the right to grow by improving customer's lives."

These are just two examples out of many. The point here is not to arrive at a precise definition, nor is it to stake a position. Rather, the point is that the multiple definitions are just the tip of the iceberg of confusion and complexity when it comes to customer success.

PURPOSE OF CUSTOMER SUCCESS

As we discussed in a previous chapter, the origin of customer success was a reaction to churn; the famous anecdote is that Salesforce was losing 8 percent of its customers per year because there was no one accountable for helping customers realize value. But today, many successful companies report retention rates well into the high 90 percent, and in a lot of cases, net retention rate (revenue from existing customers in the current year divided by revenue from the same set of customers in the prior year) is over 100 percent. This means not only are most customers renewing their contracts, but they are also spending more.

The Customer Success function is designed with certain assumptions that are tied directly to the B2B SaaS model. An executive at a company makes the buying decision, and they agree to pay a fixed amount over a fixed time frame. Using these assumptions, we design the function to maximize product usage and report back to the executive on value from usage.

There are many new business models that are becoming popular. For example, in a model called Product-Led Growth (PLG), the end user is the decision-maker. Imagine products like Zoom or Slack that are downloaded and used in a "free" model or with minimal investment by the end users. The executive buyer does not enter the picture until after the product usage reaches critical mass. In this case, the investment comes after usage, which is the reverse sequence to how we think of events in the customer lifecycle.

In usage-based models, such as Amazon Web Services, the customer makes a commitment to a certain dollar amount but does not actually pay until they use the services. In these scenarios, the incentives of both the vendor and the customer are aligned to increase usage.

But what is the purpose of customer success in PLG and usage-based models? What should be different? It goes well beyond getting maximum usage for products that a customer is paying for, and focus shifts to the additional value customers can realize from our products and additional investments customers can make. When viewed in these contexts, isn't renewal and expansion essentially another sale?

CUSTOMER SUCCESS—WHO DOES WHAT?

"Customer Success gets kicked around," Narayana says. Changes to organization structures and mandates are a constant for CS teams. Here are a few examples: CS reports to the Chief Sales (sometimes called Revenue) Officer or the CEO, CS leaders manage all post-sale activities, and CS is a stand-alone function on par with professional services. By the way, all these changes can happen at the same company over time.

Where should customer success fall in the org chart is a common question.

As CS leaders realize that their function is not well understood, they go on a journey to define a set of activities and deliverables that their teams will perform. They will also set up metrics to measure how their teams are performing, but many of these leaders are crying out for help. Remember, Customer Success has been around for about ten years now, yet there are no widely accepted processes and methodologies as with other functions, like Sales and Marketing. There is a growing need to define what "good" looks like for a Customer Success function.

Don't get me wrong—it is critical to have a well-defined operation to scale the function, but I believe that the focus has become too inwardly focused. Too much energy and resources are spent on defining the right org structure, activities, and deliverables for the function.

Too often we focus on "time to value" as a metric. The thinking goes, the faster we onboard a customer, the better. It is important to deliver value as quickly as possible, but this goal can lead us to be myopic. At ServiceNow, we spent years celebrating "go lives," or when a customer is ready to start using the application and presumably start getting value, by having a big party and cake. ServiceNow cakes became a thing, but who was thinking longer term beyond the cake?

What is the scope of responsibility of the Customer Success function? The short answer to this question is that it changes, not just from company to company but over time within a company. At Splunk, Narayana went on to build a Customer Success team that worked with their top customers. At this size and scale, his team was supporting different customers with different needs. Hiring for a complicated mix of skills while supporting the increasing number of customers is a big challenge for CS leaders.

A similar story plays out in many other companies.

Rav Dhaliwal is an investor who advises start-ups on setting up Customer Success functions. He was a CS leader at various companies before taking up his current role. In a blog post titled "The Everything Department" published on his personal Medium blog, he very aptly points out that thinking of customer success as the "job" of one department results in creating an "everything department." In his view, if a company creates a Customer Success department "purely out of a reaction to unexpected issues or organizational gaps," you end up creating a function that is responsible for all activities that don't belong or are wanted elsewhere. In essence, this contributes to the lack of a clear vision and purpose for the function.

Thinking of customer success as just another function is the root cause of this chaos.

CUSTOMER SUCCESS TOOLS

As these teams grow, they need to standardize their processes and tools. There are several companies that have built tools to cater to this growing field. Gainsight is the most well-known of the bunch, but there are well over fifty tools that call themselves "customer success platforms." If we know one thing from the last two or three decades of technology implementation, tools by themselves do not solve problems.

In response to this chaos, there are a number of smart people starting new companies. Some of these are consulting and software firms, and unfortunately, they have only led to more noise and less clarity. There are no easy answers to this problem; if there were, someone would have solved it already!

At ServiceNow, we tried these tools and then built our own solution to support the customer success team's workflow. This platform codified certain standard activities, or "plays," and tasks that the team performs. While these standardized plays and tasks help teams respond faster to very specific events, a significant portion of their activities vary from customer to customer. Bottom line is that tools are adding to the complexity of defining customer success.

METRICS FOR METRICS SAKE

Once we set up a new function, like Customer Success, it is conventional management wisdom to look for some way to measure how well the function is doing.

One of the common measures is about product usage. How many people in our customer organizations are using our product? Which features in our product are they using? This is good data, but data collection is only valuable if followed by some action. For example, Marketing can use product usage data to nudge user behavior, or Customer Success can use it to help customers mature their usage of the product.

Another common metric is Net Promoter Score, a widely accepted way to measure customer loyalty but a metric that lacks the full context. NPS uses a survey that is taken by one person in the customer organization—most commonly a senior executive. How do we measure satisfaction of others in the organization versus those who use the product day in and day out? How do we measure their excitement about the product?

WHAT SHOULD THE FUTURE LOOK LIKE?

There are two flaws in the current state that lead to a mix of confusion and complexity. First, with so much focus on defining Customer Success as a function, we have invented another silo with its own set of activities and metrics that are too self-centered. Second, the design of the function follows either a one-size-fits-all approach, which oversimplifies everything, or a "snowflake" approach, in which every situation is unique and requires a different structure. Neither of these is good for the function to scale across industries, types of products, and different customer contexts.

Before we can answer the questions about the future of Customer Success, we need to decide on the right place to focus our energy. Instead of laboring over the inner workings of Customer Success, the function, we should ask, "What is the role of everyone in customer success as the outcome?" I do not believe it is very productive to have "Is it a function or is it a mindset?" discussions or definitions.

Let me be clear, customer success is an outcome, and there are some activities that belong in a dedicated function within the organization, but other parts of the organization like Sales, Marketing, and Product, have a role to play. The challenge is to define a model where all these functions work together toward customer success.

CHAPTER 3

A NEW MODEL FOR CUSTOMER SUCCESS

"Can software vendors and other companies identify more opportunities to grow and deliver value by taking a fresh look at customer success?" That is the question asked by the author of an article titled "Introducing Customer Success 2.0: The New Growth Engine" published by McKinsey & Company in 2018. In this article, the author presents two elements that point to a cross-functional, enterprise-wide approach.

- Unified go-to-market approach
- Customer Success embedded across the organization

Today, most companies recognize the importance of customer success—so much so that many have customer success as a core value and a board-level priority.

However, these companies often fail to take concrete action around customer success, and they apply older organizational models that served them well in the pre-digital era.

In those times, the customer-vendor relationship hinged on a distinct, onetime transaction: "closing the sale." Leaders at these organizations lack the know-how to change their go-to-market approach, resulting in organizational friction and misalignment across the silos.

We touched on some of the challenges and problems with the state of Customer Success in chapter two, where we saw that there is a lot of effort to address these—let's call them—1.0 problems. But what about Customer Success 2.0? Surely, if there was a simple solution, we would have implemented it.

How can we turn the intuitive knowledge that customer success is the growth engine into action?

I believe the next generation of customer success starts by going back to the basics. If we can clearly identify who our customers are and understand their motivations for investing in our product, we will be able to define a more holistic model for customer success.

The principles in this model apply to the entire company, not just a single function. In a sense, what we need is a new way to organize and align the entire company, where every department is working toward the overall success of the customer. The first step of this model starts with establishing a broad perspective of customer success.

Some companies talk about these broader perspectives and measures, like customer lifetime value, which are good starting points, but I am yet to see any company organize their internal operating model to maximize customer lifetime value. Many processes in place today tend to overemphasize individual transactions like a sale, product implementation, renewals, etc. Internal operating models have not evolved to support a customer's entire journey and maximize value over a longer term.

One school of thought that I prefer is that every customer interaction with the brand—marketing, selling, onboarding, and support—is an opportunity to work toward customer success. One of the common terms for this end-to-end view is "customer experience," which has a lot of different connotations. Unfortunately, these terms become marketing slogans and stop short of implementing real changes to how different teams operate.

It is not that these companies want to pay lip service; instead, the leaders in these organizations lack an organizing framework. It is my goal to offer a framework to build a more customer-centric operating model that brings all teams together.

In this book, I intentionally stay away from being the arbiter of definitions of these terms, but I wanted to find a useful definition that would help us build a new model for Customer Success. I like the definition offered by Marty Kaufman, a customer experience leader. In a blog post titled "The Role of Success in Customer Experience," he states, "Customer Experience is the sum total of all interactions a customer has with your product, company, brand, and team members." This new model will help us reimagine customer success as a model that will help us keep promises. To do this, we need to look at three types of changes:

1. Customer context: rethink the foundations of customer success
2. Company context: "best fit" services model
3. Next gen capabilities: use data about customer and company context.

Many of the principles I discuss in this model are easier said than done. I will include specific actions we can take to apply these principles using real-life examples. In this chapter, we will review the elements of the model, and each subsequent chapter will delve into the details of each element and include practical advice on how to bring these elements to life.

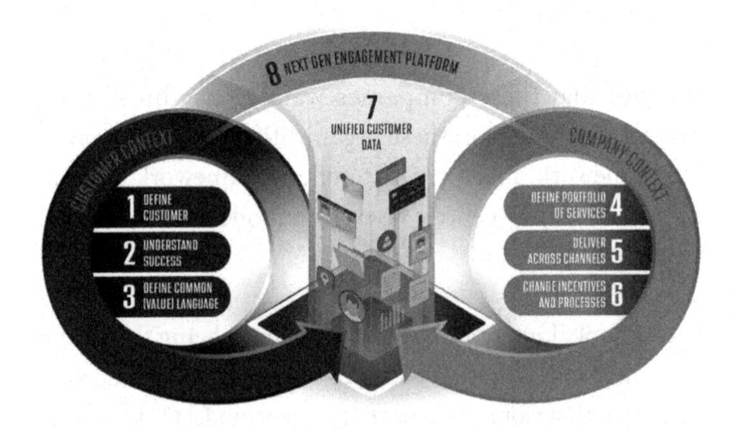

RETHINK THE FOUNDATIONS OF CUSTOMER SUCCESS

In this first part, I will challenge some of the current thinking and reframe the conventional approach to answering common questions in the customer context. As you will see, your first response to the three elements in this section may be "I've got this," and "We are already doing this." Many companies do, but their efforts are siloed across different functions. I will present an approach that leads to a common understanding of the customer that will be more holistic and unified across different teams. This approach goes beyond superficial "persona" definitions, which are commonly used by some teams to define customer characteristics. My goal is to help you validate your current approach or adjust it based on some ideas I present.

DEFINE CUSTOMER

When asked to name who the customer is, the first instinct at many companies, particularly among Sales and Marketing teams, is to think of the person who "writes the check" or those who influence the check writer. Post-sales teams, like Customer Success or Professional Services, typically think of the product's users as their customers. Neither approach is wrong, but lack of alignment contributes to the sense of confusion and complexity we talked about in chapter two.

This siloed view is not just in the vendor's organization; similar silos exist in the customer organization with a different understanding of value from a given product. Vendor teams are uniquely positioned to bring a common understanding of value and the path to realize value among the customer silos. To do that, internal teams within the vendor organizations must start with a common definition of "customer," which is the foundation of customer success.

Consider Dext, a software solution used by accountants and bookkeepers to minimize data entry by scanning financial information like expense receipts. In this case, who is the customer—the accountant who is writing the check or the small business owner who is a customer of the accountant? Consider Cisco, a large technology provider that sells their products and services through partners (other companies who work directly with customers). Are the partners Cisco's customers? The answer is that all of them are customers, in some sense, for both companies. We will explore how to define "customer" and get different teams aligned on the definition in a subsequent chapter.

UNDERSTAND SUCCESS

Once we know who the customer is, we can define what success means to them. It is important, but often overlooked, to define success in customer terms. Many Customer Success teams measure renewal rate as the ultimate measure of success. The thinking goes, "If the customer renews our product, they must be successful."

This thinking can create blind spots and focus on false positive signals. It is worth asking, "Do we really know and understand customers' motivations for using our product? Do we understand the definition of success for the full spectrum of customers?" Customer value has multiple facets—functional and emotional—similar to Maslow's hierarchy of needs. Using a *Jobs to be Done* framework, we can truly understand success for each individual customer. In a subsequent chapter, we will go into different ways to define, measure, and track success.

At CEB, we helped executives improve the performance of their departments by teaching the best practices implemented at their peer organizations. We had to understand what success meant for each executive and their teams and deliver personalized advice that was relevant to their context. While there were patterns we could draw, no two customers defined success the same way.

DEFINE COMMON LANGUAGE

Just as we discussed that customers have different definitions of success, there are different definitions of value a company is offering. Each department has their own perspective on what value we offer and how we deliver that value. Beware! On the surface, it seems like all the departments are in sync, but peel back a layer or two, and it becomes obvious that they are not speaking the same language.

Customer value promised in the sales cycle is not the same as the value product teams have in mind, which is different from how customer success teams measure value. This is not an uncommon scenario at many companies. This disconnect results in issues like poor adoption, renewal, and customer satisfaction.

This element of the model will show what a common language looks like, how it can be used across the different teams, and most importantly, what it takes to create and foster the common language. We will review examples of companies that use the common language of customer value throughout the customer lifecycle.

DEFINE BEST FIT SERVICES MODEL

The elements we outlined in the foundations section, especially the common understanding of customer and success, are just that: a foundation. It is becoming increasingly clear that customer success is not just a post-sale activity or function. In response, many proclaim that customer success is a company-wide mindset and that it is "everyone's job." In this part, we will explore elements within the company context that offer practical guidance on how to put the mindset into action.

DEFINE PORTFOLIO OF SERVICES

A deep understanding of both customer and success will make it clear that we need a portfolio of services to deliver customer success. Many companies develop different services as a natural part of their evolution. As their products mature and their customer profile changes, they realize customer needs evolve, and in reaction, they build different capabilities. I will present a more proactive approach to defining service offerings and how to match offerings to the company context.

In this section, I propose an expansive definition of services beyond the conventional understanding, which is limited to post-sale customer interactions. For example, I argue that developing marketing campaigns is as much a service as product implementation.

DELIVER ACROSS CHANNELS

It is common to think of a company website or a knowledge base on a support site as channels. A Customer Success

Manager (CSM) or an implementation team are also channels to deliver different aspects of success to the customer. These are different channels that customers interact with to get the help they need to succeed. However, there is often confusion between services and channels. Once we separate the services from channels, we can be smart about optimizing the right elements of customer experience and help them succeed. In this chapter, I will present some frameworks that will help design the best customer success model.

Let's look at some of the ways CEB's customers consumed the product (in this case, best practice research): they could visit the website to download the research studies, they could have a consultant present the research in a team meeting, or they could attend a networking event to interact with their peers. It was important for us to know which customers valued which channels so we could meet the customer where they were.

CHANGE INCENTIVES AND PROCESSES

It is not enough to set up a common language, and top-down mandates are often ineffective. The problem is misaligned incentives and established ways of working. Imagine if the Sales team gets paid when the customer renews their contract rather than at the initial sale, or the Marketing team gets paid based on product adoption, or the Customer Success team gets paid based on sales leads. How would these teams' activities change?

I realize those are radical proposals, and to be honest, they are too disruptive in one fell swoop. The point is that incentives drive action, and we will explore what kind of tactics can be used to drive different behaviors among these teams. We will look at ways to encourage different teams to walk in lock step, talk the same language, and work toward the same goals.

NEXT GEN CAPABILITIES

Activities described in the first two parts of the model will help us get a true 360-degree view of the customer. There are two next generation capabilities that we can build to truly scale customer success, but we are in the very early stages of building these capabilities.

UNIFIED CUSTOMER DATA

Use of customer data to drive higher revenues and deliver a better customer experience is table stakes in the consumer product space. Think about the ads we see on social media or product placement in grocery stores; they are all based on insights derived from customer data. In the enterprise technology space, use of customer data is in the nascent stages.

In this element of our model, we will explore how different companies are using customer data, consider what the pitfalls and opportunities are, and look at examples of leading practices.

NEXT GEN ENGAGEMENT PLATFORM

The biggest challenge for customer success, beyond solid foundations and breaking down silos, is scaling the model across the broad spectrum of customers and their needs. It's not just that it is hard to scale; we also need to change the model as products and companies mature and customer needs change. Using customer data and delivering customer success in a digital medium is the next major leap companies need to take. In fact, many artificial intelligence and machine learning technologies can be used to deliver a scalable, yet personalized, customer experience.

In this chapter, we reviewed the model that helps us organize the entire organization around customer success. When this model is implemented, customer success will be more than a department; it will be everyone's job, where different functions are aligned around common goals. My goal was to build a model that is less "ivory tower" and more practical. One can consider each element of the model, take specific actions, and see value in making changes. This framework will help align different leaders and serve as a conversation guide to set strategic priorities. In the next few chapters, we will dive deeper into each of the elements of the model and offer ways to think about each element using interesting stories from a varied set of companies and practitioners.

PART 2

WHAT IS IN THE NEW MODEL FOR CUSTOMER SUCCESS?

CHAPTER 4

DEFINE CUSTOMER

Who is your customer? The answer to this question is not as straightforward as one would think.

Imagine asking this question in a typical strategic planning meeting of a SaaS company. You will get a range of answers. Sales teams will talk in terms of buyers and influencers, Marketing teams will talk about buyer personas, Product teams will talk about user personas and roles, and Customer Success teams will talk about executive sponsors and users. Then there will be talk of customer segments, ideal customer profiles, and more. While these are not necessarily wrong answers, the problem is each function within the company has a slightly different answer.

For any company, "knowing your customer" is table stakes and something most companies think they have a firm handle on. After all, how can one sell products and services without knowing the customer? Let us look at a couple of scenarios that I came across in my research.

Jen Chiang is the director of Customer Success at Yup, a math tutoring app, and the author of *The Start Up's Guide to Customer Success*. In our interview, she said, "Our Sales team is constantly iterating on who they are selling to. They may try community colleges instead of high schools, which is our main customer segment."

That is what you would expect the Sales team to do—push the envelope and find new buyers. Other teams in the company, like Marketing and Customer Success, will need to change what they do and how they do it for each new type of customer. For example, what does it mean to implement the tutoring app at community colleges? The teachers and students at high schools and community colleges are quite different. The students at a community college could be a mix of young adults and working professionals, and there are more adjunct teachers. Does that change anything?

Another common scenario plays out something like this: if you ask a product manager at any company, "Do you know who your customers are?" they will most likely give you a list of customer personas and use cases; this is their view of who their customers are and why the customers use their product. If you then walk over to the Customer Success team and ask, "What are your common reasons for churn?" the answer is usually, "We are selling to the wrong customers."

Why is there such a disconnect?

Different teams across the company have their own idea of who the customer is, and they arrive at this idea from their unique perspective. To make it worse, each unique definition of the customer, why they buy the product, and how they use the product changes regularly, and different teams don't stay in sync with these changes.

In this chapter, I offer a few different ways to look at the customer definition. A suggested way to use this framework is to have different teams—Sales, Marketing, Product, and Customer Success (including Success, Services, and Support)—come up with a common definition of different types of customers. They can then use that understanding to develop common approaches to address the needs of these customers.

WHAT ARE THE CHALLENGES WITH HOW WE TYPICALLY DEFINE A CUSTOMER?

The most common approach many companies take is to segment customers by revenue and industry. It is common to see sales teams dedicated to selling to mid-market companies (those with less than a billion dollars in revenue, even though this definition changes across companies) or enterprise customers (companies with more than a billion dollars in revenue). There are also some teams focused on certain markets, such as healthcare, government, education, etc.

It is a sound approach to understanding trends in these segments and applying different techniques to engage these customers. However, this segmentation is used primarily in the sales process. Other functions do not always find this segmentation useful.

Another approach that is common is to develop an "ideal customer profile." This describes the customers who are most likely to buy and use the company's products. The problem with this approach is that it is only effective for an individual product, and even then, not in all cases. What happens when a company sells many kinds of products, and customers use the product to solve different problems than the company intended? Last but not least of the problems is that the ideal customer profile is not static, and it changes as the company grows.

All these approaches miss the fundamental, human element of the customer. They help us design our internal teams and processes but miss the mark on truly understanding the customer, their needs, and motivations.

BUYER *VS.* DEPLOYER *VS.* USER

A sale is usually a promise to deliver value in return for investment, and there are different people involved in making and keeping that promise. A typical enterprise software sales process goes something along these lines: The salesperson builds a strong relationship with an executive, learns their business challenges, proposes the solution they (the salesperson) are selling, and convinces the executive to write the check. The executive is the buyer.

The buyer then brings in their team to implement the solution. Let's call this team, or individual, the deployer. Once implementation is complete, the solution is deployed to others in the organization, who are the users of the solution. The gist of this scenario is that it is important to have a clear understanding of all these moving pieces.

Rav Dhaliwal is a former CS leader and currently an investor and venture partner at Crane, a London-based venture capital firm. Rav and his team work with hundreds of start-ups and understand what separates those that are successful from those that are unsuccessful. He summarized his observations in a blog post titled "There Is No Such Thing as Post Sale," stating, "These companies have realized (and accounted for) the fact that there is often a very big difference between the buyer (who definitely has specific outcomes in mind) and the people tasked with deploying and eventually using the software (the "deployer").

This is particularly true when a vendor offers many products, and the customer has bought more than one. Imagine the company I work for, ServiceNow. We have several products to manage workflows across several parts of an IT department, each with its own unique users. Our products are used by help desk operators, project managers, and IT administrators—among others. We also offer products used by Human Resources teams, Customer Service teams, and many others.

The problem of buyer *vs.* deployer is pronounced for my company, ServiceNow, as will be the case for any company with many different products bought and used by different people. In ServiceNow, there are various combinations of buyers, users, and deployers, and not all of them are part of the same conversations, nor do they all have the same motivations in relation to adopting our products. In his aforementioned blog post, Rav goes on to say, "Understanding the 'distance' between the purchaser and the deployer/end user and preparing to close it *during* the sales process is something each of these companies do particularly well."

Rav and his team's experience highlights the need for understanding the different postures that buyers and deployers take toward adopting the product. In a similar vein, product users should be treated as different-in-kind customers. The first step to understanding the "distance" between these customers is to build a common understanding among different functions, like Sales, Marketing, Product, and Customer Success. This way the entire company can take steps to understand and address the needs of these customers.

PROSPECT *VS.* CUSTOMER

The most common growth model in SaaS companies today is to sell one of your products to a customer and then sell other products to expand the company's footprint. This model is commonly known in the industry as "land and expand."

Sales and Marketing teams at most companies use the phrase "buyer's journey" to define a series of interactions that potential buyers, called "prospects," have with the company. These journeys document the key questions that a customer might ask at each stage of the journey and the company's answer. Amanda Sellers presents a good example of a buyer's journey in a blog post titled "What Is the Buyer's Journey?" on HubSpot's (a popular marketing automation software) website. There are three stages in the journey:

- Awareness
- Consideration
- Decision

Many of these journeys are built with a new prospect, not an existing customer, in mind. In most cases, the company does not know a lot about the prospect. But in the "land and expand" model, the company knows a lot of contextual information about the customer. What does the buyer's journey look like for a prospect who happens to be a customer? How can we engage these prospects differently?

Marketing teams create content to entice a prospect to be interested in the products of the company. They try to convince them of the value proposition using this content. Similarly, Customer Success teams build content to help customers implement and use the product. In most cases, these two types of content are completely different. This difference reflects the silos within the company. In my experience, Customer Success content can be very useful for marketing purposes as the customers feel more confident in the company's ability to support them after the sale.

My team at ServiceNow recently published a new document type called Success Map. Within the document, we outlined the activities a customer should perform to successfully adopt a product, including activities after the implementation, like defining the right roles. The last step in this map was a recommendation for the next set of products to implement. Not surprisingly, our Sales teams find this document to be extremely valuable for two reasons. One, they can build credibility with the customer by helping them successfully (and quickly) implement the first product that the customer bought. Two, they can set up the next sale as a natural extension of the first sale and implementation.

It is in the best interest of both the customer and vendor to use the information they know about each other to expand the relationship; this makes the process less of a transaction and more like a relationship you are navigating.

CUSTOMER'S CUSTOMER

In some cases, the end user of the product is the customer of the company that is buying the product; I will call this group the end user throughout this chapter. The value of the product to the company that buys your product is directly dependent on the value to the end user.

Nora Khalili, who runs a consulting practice advising startups on their CS strategy, makes defining customer value a central piece of her advice. When I interviewed her, she talked about a previous role at Dext, a receipt scanning software for small accounting practices. Nora says, "The hardest part was to get accountants' customers [small business owners] to scan the receipt. That was the biggest struggle." Small business owners have to change how they do their work, scan receipts as they come in instead of saving them and sending the stack to the accountant.

In this case, even though the accountants were paying for the software, the real customer was the small business owner—the end user of the software. When Nora's team realized this, they changed their marketing to highlight the benefits for small business owners. Their pitch changed from, "We will save you [the accountants] time" to "Look at the efficiency gains for this accountant's customer! They spend less time on tracking receipts and more on growing their business."

They went so far as to call the end user their client and the accountants their partners.

Another example is from an interview I did with Faisal Raza, VP of Customer Success for Ionic, back when he was with a different company called OPower, which is now part of Oracle. OPower's solution was sold to utility companies with a goal of changing customers' power usage habits. To do this, they had to change how information was presented in the customer's utility bill. OPower's solution was indirectly used by the utility's customer. Raza told me that the implementation teams had to engage with the Marketing and Public Relations teams of the utility companies because the utility bill is viewed as customer communication. Without fully understanding this context, implementation teams might be ill-prepared to work with and satisfy the needs of the Marketing teams.

The focus on the customer's customer will be even more important in the future as all enterprise software companies extend their products to serve the eventual "consumer" of their customers' products.

These three ways of defining the customer are by no means exhaustive, but they provide a good starting point to understand our customers. One common theme across the three customer definitions is the intimate knowledge that the vendor has of the customer's business and the context in which they operate. It is not just important for one part of the organization to have this deep understanding of the customer. It is equally, if not more, important for different parts of the organization to have this common understanding. This knowledge of the customer will pave the way to the next element in the framework, which is understanding what success means for each of these customers.

CHAPTER 5

UNDERSTAND SUCCESS

What exactly is success? And whose success are we referring to?

Success can be defined in many ways. As HubSpot co-founder Dharmesh Shah shares in a blog post, "Success is making those who believed in you look brilliant." Looking "brilliant" has two forms—one can look brilliant in their role as an individual or as a member of an organization.

It is common to tie success measures to organizational or team-level measures, like reducing costs or improving revenue. This overlooks the benefit to the individual, which leads to issues like low product adoption and resistance to change. Sometimes the personal-level success measures and organizational-level success measures do not align. Merely acknowledging that fact will help us take better, more informed actions.

In a *Harvard Business Review* article titled "The Elements of Value," the authors state that what customers "truly value, however, can be difficult to pin down and psychologically complicated." They categorize elements of value in a hierarchy that mirrors Maslow's hierarchy of needs, a famous idea in the field of psychology.

Maslow's hierarchy of needs was proposed by Abraham Maslow in his 1943 paper "A Theory of Human Motivation." According to this idea, human needs are presented in a pyramid form with basic needs—like physiological and safety needs—at the bottom, followed by psychological needs—like belonging, love, and prestige—in the middle, and self-actualization needs at the top.

The authors of the *HBR* article categorize the thirty elements of value into a pyramid with four categories: functional, emotional, life changing, and social impact. In B2B companies, we focus a lot on functional value—reduce costs, save time, make money, etc.—and much less on the other three categories.

I found there are a lot of definitions of customer success, and most of them have a very narrow focus on functional value or are very vague. Few define success of the customers at a human, emotional level. In this chapter, we will investigate different ways of defining success and the pitfalls of some of the tactics we use to define success. We will also explore factors that contribute to success and how companies can home in on the most important factors.

JOBS TO BE DONE

Defining success is not a new problem that organizations face. After all, it is widely accepted that making customers successful is the pathway to a company's success.

I found the "jobs to be done" framework, discussed by the renowned management thinker Clayton Christensen, in his book *The Innovator's Dilemma.* Christensen is well-known for his work in disruptive innovation and introduced jobs to be done as an essential component of innovation.

In the article "Know Your Customers' 'Jobs to Be Done [JTBD],'" from *Harvard Business Review*, the authors write the following: "What [firms] really need to home in on is the progress that the customer is trying to make in a given circumstance—what the customer hopes to accomplish. This is what we've come to call the *job to be done.*" Despite knowing a lot about customers today, companies fail to target innovations that help customers because they rely on correlations that do not highlight the real needs of the customer.

Tony Ulwick, founder of the strategy and innovation consulting company Strategyn, is one of the pioneers to apply the JTBD framework to an innovation process, which he calls Outcome-Driven Innovation. Typically, JTBD is used to define product and business model innovation. I believe the same principles can be applied to achieve customer success.

According to a playbook published by Strategyn, "Jobs are functional—with emotional and social components." This thinking is in line with article titled "The Elements of Value" that we discussed earlier. We often fall short of understanding all components of all jobs of all customers. Other tenets Strategyn lists are that "Jobs are stable over time" and "Jobs are solution agnostic."

To apply this framework in the context of customer success, we start with understanding the motivations and needs of each type of customer. For this, we must go beyond the standard customer segmentation techniques and understand customer needs more deeply.

I am giving a cursory treatment to a sophisticated concept and practice here. Understanding customers' jobs to be done is not easy. It requires a carefully thought-out approach and maybe help from folks who have done this before.

First, I must issue a disclaimer: I am using Strategyn's material for my research, but there are others who claim to have invented this framework. A Medium article titled "Confused About Jobs to be Done? So Was I." presents the two main applications of this framework. For purposes of my argument in this chapter, I find the core principles useful irrespective of how they are applied.

I interviewed Marty Kaufman, who was the vice president of Customer Experience at WeddingWire and now advises companies on improving Customer Experience. WeddingWire, now part of a new company, The Knot Worldwide, is a marketplace for engaged couples to select vendors for their wedding. In our conversation, Kaufman described an offsite meeting with the company leadership where the facilitator asked, "Who is your customer?"

The facilitator divided the room into two sides. He asked the participants who thought the vendors were the customers to move to one side and those who thought the engaged couples were the customers to the other side. Marty says, "I was the only one that refused to pick a side of the room." His view is that it is not an "either/or" proposition.

Most common customer segmentation techniques are based on the dollar amount the customer spends or the size or industry of the company. Marty prefers to "segment customers by their need of us." In other words, Marty realizes that each of these customers has a different job to be done, and that should drive our actions.

In the case of WeddingWire, success for an engaged couple is a seamless process to search and select vendors. Success for these couples would be measured by the choice of vendors as well as the ease with which they can hire the vendors and plan the wedding. This is the functional value of the platform for the engaged couple. There are other emotional and life changing aspects of planning a wedding that come into the picture. On the other hand, vendors measure success by their ability to run and grow their businesses using the platform. Different kinds of customers see value from different perspectives—vendors see the functional value, and the engaged couples see the functional and emotional value. We could break it down further and realize that vendor size also influences what they (vendors) need from the company (WeddingWire). Smaller vendors, such as a small farm that hosts weddings, may need help marketing their services while big vendors, such as a hotel chain, may need help with data analytics.

CUSTOMERS MAY NOT KNOW WHAT SUCCESS MEANS

A rookie mistake that most of us make, at least once in our careers, is to assume that customers will tell us their definition of success. The general line of thinking goes something like, "Customers are the experts at their business. They surely know what they want." So, we start customer engagements with open-ended questions, like "What are your outcomes?"

Thinking back to my time at CEB, my team and I had to answer some of the same questions. I remember our very first customer (a big bank) and how excited we were to get started. My contact at the bank, Amit, was very excited to show his manager the wonderful things the new software could do.

We worked feverishly for a few weeks, collecting data, organizing spreadsheets, and uploading data. After all the work, Amit came back with a question I will never forget. "Now what?" he said. "What is all this telling me?" After a few more "Now what?" discussions with other customers, we knew that we had to answer that question first before we started working with customers.

We had to be very prescriptive about the outcomes we were delivering for the customer. We defined a set of fifteen to twenty outcomes our software could help with, and we used those as the anchor for all our customer interactions. We designed an onboarding process, implementation guides, and quarterly check-ins around this menu of outcomes. This list of outcomes was so powerful we even used it in our sales process, so customers came into their post-sale process having done "homework," and we were able to deliver value faster.

Many Customer Success teams make it a priority to develop a point of view on defining success for the customers. Another example of this practice came up when I interviewed Stephen Horning, VP of Customer Success at Pantheon, a web operations platform. When he took his role, he set out to understand "What are the habits of a successful web-ops practice?" He felt it was imperative to have this point of view to make Pantheon stand out in a crowded market of web hosting platforms.

In some ways, what Pantheon offers is a commodity product—a web hosting service, but their customers expect prescriptive advice on improving their capability to manage websites. To meet this expectation, Stephen and the team are working on a WebOps maturity model by using customer usage data. This model is used to guide customers to be more productive and innovative in managing their websites.

This WebOps maturity model can be used to chart out a series of successful events in their journey together. In this case, Pantheon is helping customers by defining success on their behalf.

Customers have many choices for technology solutions these days, and the vendors who come with a complete "package of help" get ahead in the line. Customers' expectations are not limited to great products; they are looking for a great service to help them be successful. The "service" part of SaaS plays a big role in defining success for the customers who are paying for the outcomes. In other words, customers are not looking for technology. They are looking to do their jobs. Customers measure success based on their ability to get things done, and if it takes technology and service, that is what the offer should be.

MOMENTS OF TRUTH INFORM SUCCESS

The "menu of outcomes" approach helps to speed up the onboarding process, which is an important milestone in customers' relationship with the vendor. However, success is not a onetime event, and it is not always measured in post-sale interactions. There are several moments throughout the customer journey that are moments of truth when a customer makes a "go" or "no-go" decision.

Most enterprise products need some level of implementation effort to set up the solution to meet a specific customer's needs. The end of these implementation projects is a good example of the moments when success is experienced for the first time. At ServiceNow, there is an informal tradition of celebrating the end of these projects with a "go live" cake. A successful "go live" is just one measure of success.

There are other scenarios where the end of the implementation project does not by itself represent success. Brightfield, a workforce analytics company, provides insights into how companies spend on an extended workforce, like outside contractors and consultants. To generate these insights, they need to categorize customer data into their frameworks and structure.

The moment of truth for Brightfield's customers is when they see the results of the analysis and receive expert, prescriptive advice on a way forward. The Customer Success function, in this case, focuses on generating insights and recommendations from the data and lets the Product team take lead in the data integration portion.

These moments don't always happen in the post-sale portion of the customer journey. Understanding the value proposition of your product or service is one of the first moments in the customer journey that informs the customer's success. In that case, success is delivered by the positioning and messaging for the offering.

COMMON PITFALLS IN DEFINING AND MEASURING SUCCESS

In most companies, Customer Success teams are tasked with and held accountable for delivering and measuring customer success. This "throw it over the wall" approach by itself is problematic, but we will address the role of other functions in a different chapter. Some of the metrics that Customer Success teams track are inward-focused and do not reflect customer success. Let us look at some of the methods used to measure value.

VALUE REALIZATION MODELS

Value realization, sometimes referred to as benefits realization, has been the holy grail of defining success and proving value from investments. In the days of traditional packaged software, organizations invested massive resources defining sophisticated models to prove the value of investments. These models required a lot of data and highly skilled finance professionals to prove the benefits of an investment.

The effort and resources needed to use these complex models may be justified for large investments. I say "may" because the models give a sense of false precision. Investing in building these frameworks and models is not for everyone. Even large projects fall short of having the right data to calculate value in dollar terms, and sometimes the benefits are hard to quantify.

These frameworks are not always effective in measuring emotional elements of value. The biggest drawback of the models in use today is that they are done in a silo. We will look at a better way to build and use these models in the next chapter.

Another approach can be to use simple surveys or interviews to document perceived value. Christian Conti, who runs the EMEA supply chain practice at Gartner, told me in an interview that they just ask the customer to describe the value after a major initiative—for example, in projects where Gartner's consultants help the customers with the contract review process, helping them renegotiate costs. At the end of the project, they interview the customer to understand how the consultant helped them bring down the cost. The customer feedback in these interactions can serve as powerful proof of value realization.

FOCUS ON ACTIVITIES

This approach is common at many Customer Success teams where they take a "check the box" approach to completing a set of tasks as soon as they start working with the customer. Examples of these tasks include setting up a new customer, completing a customer success plan, and conducting quarterly business reviews.

Completing these activities in no way represents success for the customer, nor are they useful to understand how well the Customer Success function is working. It is better to tie the activities to success measures as defined by the customer. This requires a deeper, more thorough understanding of the customer's definition of success or the jobs they are trying to do.

PRODUCT USAGE AND ADOPTION

This is another common area where there is an inward focus, and correlations in data are given more weight than they are worth. Today's technology makes it easy to track data on how customers are using products and correlate this information with other metrics, like renewals or customer satisfaction. A big assumption behind this approach is that customers are following the vendor's intended use for the product.

Product usage data in isolation lack context and don't tell the full story behind usage. This is the point about correlations that Clayton Christensen makes in his jobs to be done article. Often, we arrive at the usage metric based on which features we want customers to use rather than on those that benefit the customer. By taking a customer-first perspective, we will be able to nudge customers toward product features that will advance their jobs.

In the case of Pantheon, the web hosting platform mentioned earlier, imagine tracking product usage that correlates to the maturity of customer's web operations. By tying it to the maturity model (described earlier in the chapter), Pantheon teams can infer when the customer is ready to move along the maturity curve to the next level.

CUSTOMER SURVEYS

Surveys are another way companies collect data to understand their standing with customers. Net Promoter Score (NPS) and Customer Satisfaction (CSAT) are two of the most popular metrics that companies use. These metrics provide a good indication of the health of the customer relationship in the customer's voice. The problem with these is that they are backward-looking and only give the perspective of one individual or, in some cases, a handful of individuals.

Shreesha Ramdas, co-founder of Strikedeck, a Customer Success software, wrote a blog post titled "Is Net Promoter Score Good Enough to Measure Customer Happiness?" In this post, he says, "NPS is rather less reliable to measure customer happiness, as there is no space to provide personal insight, express views, or provide context via comments. Unfortunately, with NPS's format limitations, there is insufficient input to predict or understand the customer experience at a deeper level."

The important lesson about customer surveys is not that they are not useful, but they need to be supplemented with other contextual customer data. For example, if we can use insights from NPS data combined with other information we know about the customer, we can change our customer interactions to avoid bad scores in the future.

BOTTOM LINE—UNDERSTANDING SUCCESS

Understanding what success looks like for customers is not easy and requires a deep knowledge of their needs and motivations at emotional and functional levels. Unfortunately, there are no shortcuts or miracle technologies that will help us define success. Different approaches used today—like customer surveys, value models, etc.—fall short of getting to a full understanding of success as defined by the customer.

The *jobs to be done* framework is useful to understand the success of the customers. I believe understanding the jobs, customer outcomes at functional and emotional levels, and the circumstances in which the customer is trying to do the jobs will enhance our understanding of success. The good news is that the companies have this information based on all the interactions customers have with the companies—it's just buried in the silos. We must look into and across silos and make it a priority and a habit to define success.

Building a common definition and understanding of success across different teams, like Sales, Marketing, Product, and Customer Success, will allow us to speak a language that appeals to the customer. This common understanding of customer and success will form the foundation for building a more effective operating model within the company. But first we need to codify our understanding of what success means to our customers in a language that all the teams use. In the next chapter, we will review what this common language looks like and how to define it.

CHAPTER 6

DEFINE COMMON LANGUAGE

In an interview, Ragy Thomas—CEO and founder of Sprinklr—told me, "My vision is to create the world's most loved enterprise software company. If you don't deliver what you promised [to your customers], you're not going to be the world's most loved enterprise software company." Keeping promises is a common theme that I heard from different companies who invested in defining common language used by all their teams. Once we define our customers and understand success on their terms, the next step is to define a common language that everyone, both different functions within the company and customers, can agree on.

Sprinklr is a customer experience platform, built for "breaking down silos" by creating what the company refers to as a unified platform for customer experience management (unified-CXM) that brings all customer-facing teams together. According to their website, these teams "use Sprinklr to market, advertise, research, care, and engage consumers across twenty-three social channels, eleven messaging channels, chat, SMS, and email." Of course, as a big fan of breaking down silos, I was happy to learn more about this company.

In another example, I interviewed Liz Gilliam, director of Marketing at WalkMe. "Value we pitch is value we deliver" was the motto for a cross-functional team that Gilliam led to define a common language across the teams at WalkMe. Most of us have used web-based or mobile applications with step-by-step guides that walk you through different features. WalkMe offers the product used to build those guides with a goal of increasing product adoption.

Gilliam and other leaders at WalkMe saw the need for helping the customers measure and share the value with the executives who approve spending on WalkMe. To support this need, leaders at WalkMe built a value framework. Once they built a framework to show the value of their solutions, it became the go-to option for customers who needed to justify renewing the product as well as for those who wanted to expand usage. Internally, this model was used by sales and post-sales teams as the common language to interact with the customer.

Once this common language is set up, it becomes the most useful resource for different teams, but getting there is not always easy. First, organizations don't see the need for this common language until they are in a crisis mode, typically when facing customer churn. Even when they see the need, getting alignment across different teams is not easy. In this chapter, we will look at how a few companies went about defining a common language and how they made it a standard way of doing business.

THE NEED

I learned about Sprinklr's value realization model from a fellow author, Asha Aravindakshan, a customer experience leader who was part of a cross-functional team that built the model. To understand how they identified the need for this model, I was lucky to talk to the top guy who spearheaded this effort, CEO and founder Ragy Thomas.

He says the value realization model was "a way to bring my company together across our silos and everyone to use the same language and everyone to have the same shared understanding with the customer." Ragy and his executive leadership team realized that to help their customers break down silos, they needed to break down the silos within their own company.

Of course, the need does not always start with the CEO initiating a project as Ragy Thomas did at Sprinklr, and that is okay. Gilliam told me that Customer Success leaders at WalkMe saw that their customers, even the happiest ones, were finding it difficult to communicate the value from the WalkMe platform. This was critical for renewing customer contracts and expanding the use of the product within a customer.

This need first surfaced in CS interactions with their customers and expanded as the company grew. At first, as these needs came in, customer success teams were building custom-made models to help individual customers. After a while, the CS leaders realized they needed a model that was consistent and could be used across all customers by all the customer success teams. Gilliam got tagged to lead this effort to build a model, and she had the full support of the leadership team beyond CS and Marketing.

As the customer interacts with different teams in the company, they see and hear different language about the value of the product—from how the company talks about its products on its website, to how Sales teams present the value proposition, to how Customer Success teams discuss expected business outcomes. When the customer uses the product, they don't have a way to tie the product usage to the value that was promised in other interactions.

What companies like Sprinklr and WalkMe do differently is communicate the value of the product consistently throughout the journey. There is a high degree of alignment around customer value and how it is communicated by various teams, like Marketing, Sales, Product, and Customer Success.

THE PROCESS

Talking to different companies confirmed that building a common language, by its very nature, takes a cross-functional team. It is not an easy feat to bring a team of folks from different departments together, especially when there is no incentive to do so. Frankly, not all the teams come on board from the beginning. The need for this common language usually starts with the post-sales services teams.

The symptoms of this problem show up after the sale in form of poor product adoption, difficulty implementing the product, or customers not being able to prove the value of the product. Many of these fall into the laps of Customer Success teams. By the time there is enough data to realize there is a pattern, there is in fact already a crisis: a crisis of churn. Since these problems come to light in post-sales, leaders at the company look to the Customer Success or other service teams for solutions. Gilliam told me that the value framework was a critical piece in not just avoiding the problem of churn but also expanding customer relationships.

A common approach to solving these challenges is to understand the problems customers expect to solve with the product and write down these outcomes that customers value. This information is commonly referred to as the value realization model, the value blueprint, or something similar. Then, CS or service teams help get customers to these outcomes.

It is not that CS teams are the first to talk the "value" language with the customer; Sales and Marketing teams develop the value proposition language to use in their interactions too. From a customer perspective, answering "What does value mean for you?" with CS teams feels like repeating the same story again to another team from the same company. The value language used in the sales process does not always include the implementation considerations. That disconnect in how different teams communicate and engage the customers leads to frustration all around.

The right way to build these value models is to think of it as the language all internal teams use among themselves and with the customers. Smart leaders know that this alignment is important. That is the reason Thomas from Sprinklr saw unified language as a must-have for the company to realize their vision. The internal structure and incentives often get in the way of building and using a common language. So, support from senior leaders, like the CEO and other C-level leaders in the organization, is critical for the success of these initiatives.

Getting all teams to use this common language is the hardest part as it requires bringing them along on the journey. They all need to see the value of adopting this language in meeting their objectives. It is easier to start with a small group to test how the common language improves their job. The WalkMe team brought a small number of their customers to help build the model, which helped different teams buy into the value of their model. The next evolution of these models is to make them available in self-service channels, where customers can learn about the models and select which part of the model applies to them. This gives the Sales and Services teams a head start in helping customers get value from the product. The self-service can be something as simple as a website or value statements included in the product.

THE CONTENT

So, what exactly is included in these value models? We will review three different models here.

Asha Aravindakshan of Sprinklr published a blog post titled "Inside Sprinklr's Value Realization Model" that summarizes their value realization model. In this model, they have three "positive business outcomes," and each outcome has three primary business use cases. Think of each use case as a specific initiative that the customer must undertake.

From the blog post, let us look at an example. For the Modern Care product, which is used by the customer service department, a common business outcome is Increase Customer Satisfaction (CSAT). To increase CSAT, customers undertake three use cases (or initiatives), which the Sprinklr platform can help them do: retain and up-skill care agents, monitor agent-customer interactions for quality, and proactively manage PR crises.

These outcomes and use cases are mapped across four phases of the customer journey that Sprinklr teams can use: position value, discover value, implement value, and realize value. In each step, different Sprinklr teams engage the customer using different tools, but they all use the value realization model. For example, in the position value phase, Sprinklr Account teams use sales material which has primary business use cases, while the pre-sales engineering (typically referred to as Solution Consulting) team works with Account teams in the discover value phase. In the implement value phase, professional service teams deliver the Sprinklr platform as the customer envisioned in the earlier stages.

Aaron Fulkerson, general manager for Success Services at ServiceNow, saw the common language as a critical component to grow the sales and adoption of the Customer Workflow product suite. In my interview with him, Aaron shared that his team created a customer value blueprint that mapped business outcomes to use cases to product capabilities. This is similar to Sprinklr's value realization model.

In addition to the common language, Aaron created a central repository of customer data that documented the use cases that each customer was implementing. This data became a treasure trove for sales teams as they were able to go to "like-customers" and tell stories of how other customers were using the CSM product. This common language is not common just for internal teams, it's also common across similar customers.

WalkMe calls their model Digital Adoption Platform (DAP) value framework. They built this framework to help customers prove the value of using WalkMe. The framework has different metrics like CSAT, application adoption, training savings, time savings, etc. in four categories: happiness, engagement, realization of value, and operational excellence. They used this common set of metrics with all their customers, allowing them to offer a starting point for value their customers should realize.

The benefits of common language extend beyond the sales and service teams—to customers.

SUCCESS FACTORS

Defining the common language is important, but it is more important to use the common language throughout the customer lifecycle. Sprinklr, for example, uses their model for marketing, sales, implementation, and renewal conversations.

Their product features are designed around the elements of the model.

There are some common success elements across these different companies' approaches to building a common language. These elements increase the chance of creating common language frameworks and, more importantly, their adoption by different teams and customers.

1. It is important to start these efforts with the right teams in the beginning. This does not mean all the teams should be part of the effort; in fact, it is better to get only the teams that are most motivated to create these models. Typically, the best set of teams is a combination of some post-sale service and marketing teams.
2. It is useful to start small in the use of the framework. Try using this language with a small set of customers while helping them adopt the product. There are also some key interactions where this common language can be useful, like the hand off from sales teams to service teams. Use this language as an anchor to transfer the knowledge about the customer from the sales process into the post-sale process.
3. Do not underestimate the need for and value of formal communication and training. Even though creating these frameworks may feel like being bootstrapped or "side of the desk" efforts, educating different teams on these frameworks should include formal communications, preferably by senior leaders and training.

A common language across different teams goes a long way in promising and delivering value to customers. However, internal structures and incentives do not support and often hinder the use of a common language, which shows up in "post-sale" problems. The root of these challenges lays not in post-sale processes, but at the beginning of customer interactions which don't start with a common, value-based language.

As with any change that impacts many teams, standard change management principles, like starting small, executive support, and widespread communication, are critical to successful adoption. Lastly, to sustain the use of a common language, look at changes needed for internal processes and incentives. We will review what these changes look like in a later chapter.

CHAPTER 7

A PORTFOLIO APPROACH TO CUSTOMER SUCCESS

Swiss Army knife. Who doesn't like one? You can do so many things with it—cut open boxes, tighten a screw on a kid's toy, open a beer bottle at a backyard BBQ, use the tweezers to pull a splinter while playing in the backyard, and on and on. It is a very useful tool to do many things. You know what it is not good for? For real, actual work. Try putting together furniture with a Swiss Army knife, and you will find out what I mean. For that, you need a set of specialized tools.

When I started working at CEB, I was the first member of the customer-facing team. Over the next year or so, we grew into a team of three people who did a little bit of everything. First and foremost, our focus was to help our customers start using the product and realize the value envisioned in the sales cycle. Then, we helped them with reports to show the value to their executives. Over time, we created standard tools and templates to help customers become more self-sufficient with minimal help from us.

We realized our customers needed "doing" help (how to use the product, navigation, and creating reports) and "thinking" help (think about the story to tell, what's a good starting point, etc.). After a year or two, my team was involved in product implementation, executive presentations, customer training, and much more. In essence, my team became the Swiss Army knife for our product.

I found that many CS leaders' and teams' experiences are not much different from this. The Customer Success function often evolves into the Swiss Army knife for post-sale customer engagement. My favorite description of this problem is what Rav Dhaliwal calls the "Everything Department." I referenced his blog post titled "The Everything Department" in chapter two.

Yes, your CS team can train your customers on how to use the product, manage the onboarding process of a new customer, and manage the renewal process. This approach might work when you are just starting off, but it is not a long-term sustainable strategy.

Each CS leader I spoke with has realized that they have continued to evolve their team's purpose, structure, and capabilities. More often than not, this change is driven by product changes (more and different capabilities) and changes in customer needs.

CUSTOMER SUCCESS—A PORTFOLIO APPROACH

One of the common questions that CS leaders ask themselves is "What should be my team's responsibility? What is in scope?" CS team responsibility does not have a one-size-fits-all answer. There are, however, some common types of services and skill sets that fall under the customer success umbrella.

Applying the *jobs to be done* framework to customer success (the outcome) will show that there are many jobs that the customer is trying to do. These jobs span the entire customer journey, starting well before the customer has formally engaged a specific vendor and going all the way past implementation. We can define a set of services that the company needs to offer to help with these jobs.

I realize that it is a big ask to rethink all 'front office' functions. According to many interviews I conducted, this approach is increasingly common in post-sale functions. Customer Success leaders and Chief Customer Officers are taking this portfolio approach to design their functions, and it's a good place to start.

I interviewed Jay Nathan and Jeff Breunsbach, the leaders of the Customer Success function at Higher Logic. Jay is the CCO, and Jeff is the director of customer experience. Jay told me, "Our professional services team had built out these fantastic packages—very repeatable and highly prescriptive—but we noticed that they (the packages) were turning over a really high rate at the end of the first year." They realized that their customers need different services from year to year, and their company needed predictable, recurring revenue.

They combined services like professional services, support, and exclusive community events into packaged service offerings. This portfolio approach not only helped post-sale teams deliver predictable business but also made it easier to get the customers ready for implementations. Jay explained, "This portfolio approach helped us decrease their average time-to-value by 40 percent."

In the rest of this chapter, I present an approach that customer success leaders can take with stories of breaking down the post-sale silos. This approach can be easily extended to all go-to-market functions by defining each of these services more broadly. There are four types of services that we can offer to the customer. It is easy to imagine these in the post-sale portion of the customer journey, but I propose that they are applicable to the entire journey.

- Relationship-based services—These services are needed to maintain an ongoing relationship with the customer throughout their journey. The purpose of these is to continuously educate the customer on the product and help them navigate their success journey. Examples of these services include the following: account management, success management, and renewal management.
- Time-bound services—These services are offered with a set start and end date, during which time the company delivers pre-defined value to the customer. The critical success factors for these services are to define the scope, timing, and outcome clearly. Examples of these services are onboarding, implementation, and product trials.
- Always on services—These services are built to provide information or help as and when the customer needs

them. These services are the most effective way to meet customer needs at scale, but they may not fit very specific needs. Examples of these services are self-service information sources like the company website, knowledge base, and user community.

- Event-triggered services—These services are used by customers based on certain events, like finding an issue with the product or a new team member joining the team. The purpose of these services is to solve very specific challenges or answer questions that "always on" services cannot. Examples of these services are technical support and training.

Companies must offer a broad set of skills and services to help customers succeed, and this combination of services varies based on the company and customer context. As the company and its products evolve, so does the need for these skills. Customer Success should be viewed as a portfolio of services and skills that are needed to help your customers. You will need a well-thought-out strategy and a deep understanding of customer context to define the right mix of services in that portfolio.

In short, we need to think of Customer Success as a set of sophisticated tools you need to build something that lasts a lifetime—in this case, a mutually beneficial customer relationship. In the next chapter, we will talk about using different channels to deliver these services depending on the context of the product and the customer. In the rest of this chapter, we will see how the portfolio approach best positions the Customer Success function to respond to changes in the company context.

CUSTOMER SUCCESS CHANGES WITH COMPANY LEVEL AND PRODUCT CHANGES

The path taken by Brian LaFaille, global head of Customer Success programs at Google, is familiar for many CS leaders. Brian joined Looker, a data analytics platform that was acquired by Google in 2019, as the first member of the CS team. At that time, the CS team was more commercially oriented, accountable for renewal and expansion of revenue. After a year or so into his role, Brian says, "We noticed that our retention numbers were good, but expansion numbers were not where they needed to be. After listening to a lot of calls, especially the commercial negotiations, we realized CSM are not the best suited for this task. In fact, we have experts at commercial negotiations. They are our sales reps."

They made the Sales team accountable for the expansion process. This allowed them to add more customers to each CSM to support. One unintended consequence of this change was that CSMs were now chasing paperwork for renewals, especially with a higher number of customers. They created a renewal operations function to manage the renewal process. This allowed CSM to focus on product adoption and customer engagement.

Changing someone's job responsibilities is not an easy task, and not all changes can be made at the same time. All these changes Brian described took place over four years. For example, they had to assure CSMs that their job responsibilities were not being cut and get the sales teams to buy into the new responsibilities. As is common in a fast-growing software company, just as we get used to one change, something else changes. This is exactly what happened when Google acquired Looker.

"We sold licenses that were between fifty thousand to one million dollars per year. That was our sweet spot. Going into Google, Looker's product was 'attached' [part of a big sales transaction] to big deals worth tens of millions of dollars." With all the changes the Looker's CS team went through, they had settled into a good rhythm of working with customers in that sweet spot. CSMs were working with data analysts or other technical teams in the customer organizations. They helped fifty to one hundred people to use their product.

The CSM role at Looker was limited to technical aspects of the product, but with larger customers at Google, the expectations were different. It was not just that Looker's teams had to train thousands of people but that customers expected advice on deeper technical topics and broader managerial topics. For example, customers would want to know how to develop analytics strategy that helps advance their company goals.

I have seen this shift at my company, ServiceNow. When we were primarily an IT help desk automation solution, our post-sale teams were expected to be technical experts who could help customers implement the product quickly. As ServiceNow became a platform with many different uses spanning all of IT, beyond the help desk, HR for employee onboarding and Customer Service departments, we saw a need to develop best practice advice on how to manage the platform. The questions were not limited to technical aspects of the product; they spanned management disciplines, like organization structure and change management.

Customer success is impacted by many factors, and they change with product offerings, changes in customer expectation, and other external events. That is where a portfolio approach offers the necessary agility to keep up with these changes.

CUSTOMER SUCCESS BY PRODUCT TYPE

Customers of enterprise software companies will need implementation service and technical support after the initial implementation. We should investigate a few other nuances around customer needs to really understand what help customers require.

I spoke to Faisal Raza, VP of Customer Success at Ionic, an open-source software platform to build mobile apps. Before joining Ionic, Faisal worked at various start-up companies that were in the growth phase and needed to scale their customer engagement functions. One of the cool companies he worked for was OPower (acquired by Oracle), a customer engagement platform for utility companies.

Faisal reiterated the importance of implementation services based on his experience at Opower. He also worked at Upskill, a company that used augmented reality—think, Google Glass-like device—to help frontline workers, like those working on a factory floor or in a retail store, like Walmart. Faisal says that, at Upskill, the "training and adoption team's job was to understand the facility that we're going to be working in, like a manufacturing floor or logistics warehouse, and help customers with questions around where the glass will be stored, how to get Wi-Fi connection to the device, etc." This required a different skill set from those of the CS team at OPower.

For products that are used by technical users, like developers and engineers, there is less of a need for implementation services. These users like to engage their peers and learn from them. So, an always-on service like a user community where they can ask and answer technical questions is a great resource.

CUSTOMER SUCCESS BY BUSINESS MODEL

Customer success came to prominence as subscription-based business models became the norm in the software industry. Over the past ten to fifteen years, this shift has become the default revenue model across industries. In these models, the revenue is still based on time-bound contracts where customers pay the vendor in regular time increments (e.g., monthly or annually). In the past few years, different variations of subscription models have come to light that require us to rethink Customer Success models.

The first of these is consumption-based revenue models. This is not a completely new concept. In the regular subscription models, there is an element of consumption that is baked in. For example, the price depends on the consumption of user licenses or features, but for the most part, there is a large, fixed element in the price. Cloud computing, where customers pay-per-use, is a common example for consumption-based models.

In a consumption-based model, Customer Success and sales processes are more intertwined than in a more traditional licensing model. In a YouTube video titled "How Microsoft is Building the World's Largest Customer Success Team," John Jester, then VP of Worldwide Customer Success at Microsoft, outlined the changes they made as part of the shift to the cloud-based model at Microsoft. They included a Customer Success team as part of their field sales teams, which in most companies include account executives and pre-sales engineers. The addition of this third member to the account team shows that they see customer success as a key piece to increase sales.

Selling products directly to end users is another emerging business model where the starting point of the sales cycle shifts from the executive, who writes the check, to the end user of the product. This is commonly referred to as product-led growth. I found the resources about PLG on the OpenView partners website to be very informative in my research.

In this model, the typical customer success approach, where value realization is a post-sale activity, breaks down. Rather, the focus is on proving value early in the engagement using a free version of the product and building up the case for the paid version of the product. In a sense, customer success comes before sale.

WHAT IS THE KEY TAKEAWAY?

To achieve customer success, companies need to develop a portfolio of services that help customers throughout their journey. This portfolio of services needs to change as the company and the product evolve, and it is heavily influenced by the business model. As with any portfolio, a services portfolio should be reviewed periodically and adjusted. In the next chapter, we will look at different models to put the portfolio together and how to adjust it over time.

CHAPTER 8

DELIVER ACROSS CHANNELS

How do we decide which services are most impactful to our customers? That is literally a million-dollar question that a lot of organizations try to answer. Unfortunately, the answer to this question consists of two words that are at the core of many a consultant's livelihood: it depends.

In this chapter, we will unpack the "it depends" answer and look at ways of deciding the right services using the right channels. Before we delve into the details of how to match customers with services to help them realize success, we should understand the mode of delivery or channels for these services.

CHANNELS—A MIX OF PEOPLE AND TECHNOLOGY

Any service you offer a customer is done so using a channel. Typically, we think of company websites, social media platforms, or events, like webinars, as the channels. This is true for one-to-many communications with customers. We can take a more expansive view of a channel by seeing it as any means we use to communicate with and engage our customers. Then there are many channels, including all customer-facing teams, such as sales, support, and customer success, and the product that customers are using.

One could ask, "What about back-office functions, like Finance, Procurement, and Legal, engaging with customers? Are they a form of a channel?" Their interactions with customers affect customer perception of our brand, but for the purpose of this chapter, we will limit the definition to all teams that are actively engaged in delivering customer value. After all, paying an invoice, as important as it is, does not represent value to the customer.

One way to think of channels is by the type of interactions they facilitate: a high touch model, where there is a higher extent of human-to-human interactions, or a low touch model, where the interactions are one-to-many. Many customer-facing teams, like Sales and Customer Success, will fall into the high touch channels, whereas the company website and the online support website fall on the low touch end. (Sometimes the latter are referred to as "tech touch" since there is no human interaction.) Marketing events, like webinars and user conferences, are somewhere in the middle.

Increasingly, the products and services themselves are a channel for communication with the customer and are an interesting combination of high touch and low touch models. The product interface and the user level data make it possible to create personalized interactions, like a high touch channel, with the scale of a low touch channel.

Implementation and reselling partners are a channel that is often overlooked at many companies. For companies that have complex products, those that require up-front implementations or large-scale change management efforts, partners are major channels through which customers experience the product. In the case of large vendors, like Cisco, a customer may never interact directly with Cisco and rather work with a partner throughout the lifecycle, from sales, to implementation, to renewal.

I interviewed Brian Foster, Customer Success leader at Appian, a low-code development platform. When he first started at Appian, Brian rolled up his sleeves to understand the biggest challenges that Appian was facing, those which would have the most impact on company growth. Brian realized that successful customer implementation is the most urgent challenge. Since IPO, Appian has been on a journey to increase the share of subscription revenue while reducing the share of services revenue.

It did not take long before Brian, along with other leaders, realized that a significant portion of partner-led implementations was failing and needed Appian's own services teams to go on course-correction missions. Low-code platforms like Appian are new to market, and many partners do not have the sophisticated skill sets needed to implement these products. There was a direct correlation between successful implementation and Appian's own services team's involvement.

Brian and his team designed service offerings for which partners can pay and get the Appian team's assistance in these activities. This was a good way to scale Appian's impact across many customers. After some trials, they arrived at two types of services. Boost Foundations, where Appian provides expert advice to partner teams, and Boost-plus, where Appian augments partner teams with additional personnel.

CS MODELS BASED ON PRODUCT AND CUSTOMER CHARACTERISTICS

In chapters four and five, we discussed the different types of customers and how each has different criteria of success. Besides customer characteristics, product-specific factors inform what services are needed to support customers' successful outcomes.

In her book, *The Startup's Guide to Customer Success*, Jen Chiang presents a Customer Success model based on Product Complexity and Customer Complexity. The focus of her framework is to help decide how Customer Success functions would operate in a company. Chiang defines Product Complexity as "how complex your product is for your customer to use." The goal is to understand how the users derive value from the product and what it takes for them to get value. Product Complexity is a factor that determines the types of services the vendor has to offer.

Implementation services are a must for products that must be customized to a specific organization's needs like the type of data entered, the specific steps in a process, and the type of management reports needed. Most workflow automation solutions, like Salesforce and ServiceNow, fall into this category. On the other hand, with a product like Calendly, which is used to schedule appointments, users can get started by just entering an email address. For such products, low touch services like web-based training and automated emails are the best services.

There are some products that are used by technical users, like developers. These products will need on-demand technical help on support websites or user communities. These products will also require thinking about online learning services that developers can use to learn new skills. In such cases, the company needs to enable these channels with the right content and services and then get out of the way of developers.

The second factor that Chiang describes is User Complexity, which describes "how deeply and emotionally your product impacts your customers." One way to think of emotional impact is to consider how much a product helps a user to complete their jobs to be done. Consider two scenarios, one where a product makes the customer's life easier and is therefore adopted enthusiastically, and the other where a customer must use the product but does not necessarily enjoy it.

Each scenario requires a different type of service and channel combination to help the user. In the first case, on-demand help content embedded in the product may be the best option because this is a scenario where the help needs to be transparent. In the second scenario, an implementation team specialized in organizational change management might need to be engaged to educate the users on the "why," "what," and "how" of the product.

Marty Kaufman, who runs a customer experience consultancy, Infinipoint, has a different variation of a model that he uses to formulate his customers' retention strategy. Marty outlined his framework in a LinkedIn post titled "3 Areas That Inform Your Customer Retention Strategy." This framework has components similar to Chiang's but with his own take: for customer dimension, he uses number of customers and their perception of value from the product. For product dimension, he uses inherent complexity, similar to what Chiang does, and the impact of the product on customer operations.

He adds a third factor to his model: the expectations of the company for the services team (which he refers to as the "retention team"), whether they are supposed to contribute revenue, and the metrics used to track the performance of the team. His point of view is that, besides the customer and product characteristics, a company's own expectations of the post-sale teams are important to define the overall customer retention strategy.

I find this thought process very useful to answer one of the controversial questions in the customer success community: "Should we charge for customer success services?" The answer is yes if the strategy of the company is to grow services revenue and the customer context demands services that customers are willing to pay for.

The moral of these frameworks, and Appian's example above, is that designing the right service offering and selecting the right channels starts with a deep understanding of the customer, their success criteria, and the product offering. This is applicable to the entire customer journey, not just post-sale services.

The complexity and variability of customer and product as well as the changing business models challenge the current siloed approaches to engage the customer. What we need is a services model that is designed and continuously calibrated to meet customers' needs in each of their interactions with the company. A services model will also make it easy to change how we deliver these services and how we measure the consumption and value of these services.

The changes needed to go way beyond minor tweaks to the existing processes. All teams involved need to work together to design and deliver these services. The post-sale teams are a good start, but we cannot stop there. That goes to the central argument of this book. As Sales and Marketing and Product teams take an active role in helping customers realize value, there is no doubt in my mind that those processes will become complex.

That is the reason most companies claim that customer success is a company-wide mindset, but putting that mindset into action is messy. There are many answers, and the answers keep changing as the company and its customers change.

WHAT IS THE TAKEAWAY?

The customer and company context inform how to package services and how to deliver them across different channels. There is no single "right" answer when it comes to delivering the right services—at least, there is no answer that doesn't change. As the company's products evolve, so do customers' needs and expectations. It is imperative to continuously evolve the service offerings and how they are delivered to the customers. At the risk of using a cliché, I propose that companies need to be agile in designing and delivering the right services across different channels.

In the next chapter, we will review the changes to incentives and work processes needed to support the delivery of these services and foster the "customer success is everyone's job" mindset.

CHAPTER 9

CHANGES TO STRUCTURES, INCENTIVES, AND PROCESSES

Incentives, especially monetary ones, are a great way to drive behavior and outcomes. The problem with the current incentive structures is they aim to optimize outcomes for each team individually.

Imagine if the Sales team gets paid when the customer renews at the end of the year, or the Marketing team gets measured on adoption of product features. What if the Product team's compensation is tied to customer satisfaction or NPS scores? How about if the Customer Success team gets paid for writing compelling marketing content? How would this change the prioritization of effort within these teams?

No, I am not suggesting a complete overhaul of compensation structures. In fact, that could be disastrous! However, we must concede that incentives should reflect and be aligned to company-wide priorities. If the company-level goal is customer success, and we know that success takes collaboration across silos, there is no better way to bring about collaboration than tweaking incentive structures.

There are many other aspects that foster collaboration including the following:

- How roles are defined
- How work processes are designed
- Tools and systems to support work
- Coaching of teams by senior leaders

In short, there are many small techniques that we can apply to drive changes in behavior. In this chapter, we will see how some companies handled changes to incentives and org structures to drive behavior change.

GOALS AND INCENTIVES

HubSpot is a "born in the cloud" company that had the benefit of defining compensation structures from the ground up and, in their early days, changing them regularly. In a talk titled "Aligning Sales, Services, and Marketing Around Customer Success" posted on the Technology & Services Industry Association's (TSIA) YouTube channel, Mark Roberge, who was then the chief revenue officer of Hubspot, details their efforts to use sales compensation plans to achieve desired behavior from their sales teams.

When they noticed that their customer churn rate was problematic, Roberge, dove headfirst into data. He wanted to understand if the performance of customer success managers (CSM) was a factor to see if some were better at serving customers than others. "If one or two figured it out, we could just copy their process," he said. Mark found no difference in churn rate across all CSMs.

He then did the same analysis by looking at sales teams. To his surprise, he found that some salespeople were better than their peers at bringing in customers who stayed with the company. He realized that "many of the churn issues were rooted in Sales rather than Customer Success." In the early days of HubSpot, they were focused on increasing their customer base and rightly so. The sales staff were compensated as long as the customers stayed with the company for four months, and the sales commission was doubled if they exceeded their sales quota.

In essence, there was a singular focus on bringing in new customers. In data, they saw customer churn going up right at the five-month mark. In Roberge's words, "Salespeople work their comp plans." This forced them to look at customer lifetime value (LTV) instead of new revenue only. They noticed even their most successful salespeople (measured by number of new customers) were signing up customers with lower LTV. So, they changed the compensation plan by rewarding sales reps who brought in customers with higher LTV.

They continued to tweak the sales plan every two years or so to adjust to the changes in customer and product mix. HubSpot and Roberge realized that "the sales compensation plan is a powerful vehicle to drive customer success." The benefit of being a young company was that they did not have to deal with the rigid organizational structures, incentive schemes, etc. that many established companies must work with.

Compensation structures are a big driver to affect behavior change and to indicate company priority. They don't have to be massive changes; rather, they can be minor nudges. It doesn't even have to be monetary.

When I interviewed Aaron Fulkerson, general manager for Customer Success offerings at ServiceNow, he told me about a customer database he created where he tied product capabilities to customer use cases. This data is a treasure trove of knowledge that sales teams can use to establish credibility with customers and to help customers match the right products to their needs. Aaron made a tacit "gentlemen's agreement" with the sales teams that they will add information about their customers to this database in return for using this data in their sales process. In this case, this was a little give-and-take that benefited both sales teams and customer success.

At Typeform, the customer marketing team's goal is to improve the percentage of customers using product features that correlate to higher retention rates. This was detailed on 'nuffsaid's website in a blog post titled "Why Customer Marketing Must Live Within Customer Success." This is different from most marketing teams' goals, which focus on generating sales leads and measure open rates for emails or website visits.

ORGANIZATION STRUCTURES

Organization structure is another powerful tool to drive changes in behavior and to signal a company's priorities. This requires breaking the mold of traditional organization structures and role definition. It is common practice to set up Customer Success as a post-sale function with a hand off from sales teams after a customer buys the product. Similarly, all marketing teams, including those that work with customers (rather than prospects), tend to be organized under Chief Marketing Officer.

When Microsoft pivoted to being a cloud-based business, it had to focus on customer success. They reorganized their customer-facing teams to include three types of teams: an Account team, which manages customer relationship, a Specialist team, which focuses on customer acquisition, and a Customer Success team, which helps customers realize value and increase consumption. John Jester details these changes in a talk titled "How Microsoft Is Building the World's Largest Customer Success Team," which was posted on Gainsight's YouTube channel. With this adjustment, Microsoft had to focus on clear role definition across these three teams, determine the right size of these teams within a business unit, and define the right performance metrics and compensation structure. They felt that this organization structure was a critical piece in their goal to be a subscription-based business.

In most companies, Marketing teams are focused on demand generation to support bringing in new customers. I interviewed Allyn Horne, who led product marketing for ad tech businesses at Amazon and Rocket Fuel, and he agrees that marketing plays a critical role in customer acquisition and retention. When he first started at Amazon, he saw that marketing was entirely focused on supporting sales teams.

He decided to reorganize the product marketing team into acquisition and retention, but he knew this change would not be easy. According to Allyn, "There is always a tension between implementing change to tell the full story *vs.* running demand generation." With correct data on revenue retention and allowing CS teams to focus on higher value tasks, there is a way to do it. He dug into the customer retention data and saw that they were leaving money on the table. He said, "We were churning six digits of revenue per week." This occurred because customers lacked understanding of the product and the benefits of different advertising media.

Customers can use different types of media to advertise—over the top or OTT (the kind we would see when watching Roku or Amazon Prime Video), display (the banners we see on websites), audio, etc. Customers need to know which media are the best ones for their needs. Any ad tech business has revenue goals for each kind of media. To meet these revenue goals, marketing and product teams define an adoption curve. For example, start with display ads, then video, OTT, and audio. How can we nudge customers along this path? Allyn saw this as the role for marketing; after all, a good marketer can tell a story and convince customers to act.

At HubSpot, Roberge did a similar analysis of how teams were organized. When looking across different functions—sales, marketing, customer success, and product—he realized that "Every function has a different idea of who our ideal customer is." For Marketing, it was the customer who clicked on an article on the website and filled out a form. HubSpot reorganized the teams with sales, marketing, and services around the type of customers, starting with the size of the company. For example, they created a team (consisting of sales, marketing, and services) focused on companies in middle market (defined based on revenue). This led to a better understanding of the customer journey by all teams and gave them flexibility to change how they engaged with the customer.

It is common to organize sales teams by company size—commercial *vs.* enterprise is the common model—but to have self-contained teams of sales, marketing, and CS is not that common. There is no doubt that changes to organizational structure are just one of the many tools available to drive the right behavior from different teams.

CHANGES FROM OWNERSHIP TO ACCOUNTABILITY MINDSET

Any organization structure inherently leads to the defining of a sense of ownership over a set of activities and outcomes. Who owns customer relationship? Who is responsible for onboarding? Who owns renewals? Looking through articles and discussion forums on customer success, we find versions of these questions over and over.

It is understandable to focus on ownership because we have more control over the outcomes of things we own. It is easy for a CSM to check the box on onboarding, and it is easy for an account manager to get the deal done. But the customer outcome gets lost in the process. Another reason for the ownership mentality is it makes it easy to perfect the activities and continue to get better. Ownership also provides a sense of job security.

Besides losing sight of the real outcome, success of the customer, ownership can lead to turf battles and finger-pointing. It is a common refrain from CSMs that they don't have a good hand off from sales with all the information needed for onboarding. A similar scene plays out when an implementation is off rails, and sales points a finger at the services teams.

Callan Carpenter, who worked with Autodesk, outlines a lot of these challenges in a presentation titled "Integrating Sales and Customer Success in a SaaS Environment" at a TSIA conference (posted on the TSIA YouTube channel). Autodesk faced challenges as they made the switch from a traditional, on-premise model to a subscription model. Carpenter and the team found that switching to an accountability mindset helped them convey the importance of meeting customer outcomes. He uses a metaphor of the crew on a military aircraft, P3 Orion sub-hunter, to describe the customer-facing team. The aircraft's mission is to hunt for enemy submarines, and the entire crew is accountable for the mission. There is a command structure on the aircraft, but the entire crew is focused on the mission and less worried about owning their piece of the job. At the end of the day, Carpenter says, "There is no such thing as one side of the plane is crashing, and the other side is not."

Besides incentives discussed in a previous section, other tactics can help drive accountability across different teams. It is not uncommon for sales teams, who are sometimes in a rush to meet their revenue goals, to bring in "wrong" customers, even with the best intentions. Mechanisms to flag these bad sales and use that information to coach the sales team are more effective than punitive measures on compensation.

In my interview with Marty Kaufman, who led Customer Experience at WeddingWire, Marty told me that the Customer Success team had the option for two "no fault" cancellations a month. A CSM can use this option when they realize that there is no plausible way to help a customer see value in their investment. In that case, customers are refunded their money, CSMs don't have to spend their limited time on these customers, and sales teams are not penalized on their commissions. Sales and CS teams would collect information on cancelled customers and use that as a coaching opportunity and to reinforce the joint accountability for customer outcomes.

Affecting behavior change is hard, especially by changing incentives, work processes, and organization structures. These changes cause anxiety and impact morale, but these are the most effective tools that organizations have to create change. Leaders across the organization share a critical role of showing empathy and clearly communicating the need for these changes. It is easier to make these changes by showing the connection between these changes and the overall mission and outcomes.

CHAPTER 10

UNIFIED CUSTOMER DATA

"Data is the new oil," is a common adage in the technology arena. Just as oil transformed and continues to play a major role in the world economy, data has the potential to transform our lives. There are parallels between data and oil in that they both have positive and negative impacts.

We can see the impacts of data on our lives already just in the last decade. As consumers of technology, many aspects of our daily lives, from what and how we buy, how we travel, and even our sources of entertainment, have been impacted by data. We are also seeing the adverse effects of data, another trait shared with oil, with increasing concerns around privacy. Companies focused on providing technology-enabled products and services to consumers are at the forefront of using data to increase the value they deliver. Netflix nailing the next set of recommended movies to watch is just a small and inconsequential example of using data.

When it comes to the use of data in a business-to-business context, and more specifically when looking to deliver customer success, we are in the very early stages. Many companies realize the power of data in helping their customers but often flounder in their efforts to make data the centerpiece of their customer experience. The go-to catchphrase for companies is getting the "360-degree view of the customer," which makes for a good marketing slogan, but bringing this phrase to life is easier said than done.

There is general recognition in the industry of the need for customer data, and there are software solutions, referred to as customer data platforms (CDP), trying to solve this need. CDP Institute, which provides "vendor-neutral information about issues, methods, and technology related to customer data management" describes the need succinctly on its website: "Today's customers simply assume that your company knows–and remembers–who they are, what they've done, and what they want, at all times and across all channels."

Data is the by-product of how work gets done; it is created by different departments as they go about their work. The siloed nature of work and customer interactions results in a bunch of "data islands" throughout the organization, making it hard to get an end-to-end view of a customer's journey. There is also a tremendous amount of unstructured data within and outside of the organizational boundaries.

In my interview with Ragy Thomas, CEO of Sprinklr, he aptly described the position in which we find ourselves with data. In his view, the data available to us within the company's systems is like water in the swimming pool, whereas the entirety of customer data is more like the water in an ocean. We are barely able to swim in the pool today; what's ahead, and where the true promise of data lies, is in our ability to navigate the ocean.

We are in very early stages of getting a complete view of customer data with more common use cases showing up in advertising and marketing in the business-to-consumer (B2C) context. Use of customer data in an enterprise, business-to-business (B2B) context, is behind the curve.

In this chapter, we will look at different types of data that are captured throughout the organization and examples of how bridging those different data silos enables customer success and better customer experiences. We will also look at some of the pitfalls along the journey of building this next generation of data capability.

DATA ISLANDS

One advantage of data over oil is that data does not need capital-and-labor-intensive systems for exploration and extraction. As technology continues to transform our lives, data (and tons of it) is generated as a natural by-product. Customers, throughout their journeys, interact with the company in many ways using different channels, and all these interactions create a lot of data. However, making the data useful—or "refining" to continue the oil analogy—is much harder.

Customer relationship management (CRM) systems are a common source for customers' demographic data, the products bought by the customer, potential opportunities for new sales, and information about in-person interactions like meeting notes, etc. Most of these interactions are manually entered by sales teams into CRM systems. This data is only as good as the rigor put in by the sales teams when entering the data.

Along the same lines, the Marketing department captures customer interactions on other channels, like emails, websites, and event attendance. This data is often integrated into the CRM system and used by the sales teams to identify future sales opportunities.

Many solutions in the marketplace today like the CDPs go one step further than CRMs in integrating data from multiple sources and retaining this data over time. CDPs aggregate data from first-party sources, such as social media, and third-party sources, like data providers. This combined view of customers is mostly used by sales and marketing teams to acquire new customers with little to no application to help customers adopt, use, and get value from the products. In fact, these efforts don't always include the data that is collected within the product, which can be a source of great insight.

As customers use products, they are inherently generating massive amounts of data and are indirectly conveying their preferences and value drivers. This data can be, and is often, used by product management teams to understand which features of the product are most used and draw correlations between product usage and customer retention and growth.

What is not common is using product usage data as an input into the sales process. This is starting to change with companies adopting a product-led growth strategy (PLG) where product usage is the driver to build a sales pipeline. PLG companies, like Slack and Calendly, target end users as the primary customers, so they can use some of the same tactics used by B2C companies.

Besides product usage, the post-sale services teams, like Customer Success, implementation services, and customer support, interact with customers on a regular basis. Some of the data from these interactions is captured in Customer Success systems like Gainsight, but that is only a small sliver. Most of the data from these interactions is buried in meeting notes, support tickets, customer surveys, and other unstructured formats.

The bottom line is that customer data is treated as a by-product of the "real jobs" of different functions across the organization, minimizing how important it is to understand end-to-end customer interactions. I believe the root cause of this devaluation is lack of ownership at the level of the senior executive, who owns collecting and disseminating customer data. This is another example of the "customer success mindset" not translating into tangible action.

CUSTOMER DATA COMING TO LIFE

My firsthand experience of using customer data in my role as the Customer Success leader at Gartner also happens to be one where we turned around a struggling business. We started with product usage data to see how well our customers were using the product. This data by itself was not very insightful and did not tell the whole story of which customers were likely to stay with us and which were at risk of leaving.

After analyzing why customers were leaving, we were able to pull together a more complete view of customer context. We used data on clarity of the customers' vision, engagement of key stakeholders, and the number of different ways the product was used. These data elements combined with product usage gave us more actionable insights to identify "at risk" customers and make sure we were able to retain them.

This practice from almost ten years ago is now commonplace at many SaaS companies, or it is at least not hard to replicate such a model. The use of customer data is a lot more sophisticated at many other companies.

"Customer experience means the perception that customers have of our brand. It is not about the functions that report to me, but it is how the whole company comes together to deliver an experience that is based on trust and simplicity. That perception of brand is impacted by every touchpoint from marketing, sales, and customer success." This is what Maria Martinez, Cisco's Chief Operating Officer, says about her role in a blog post titled "How Software Subscriptions Help Cisco Earn Its Revenue" on Salesforce's website.

At the center of Cisco's transformation is a new customer model focused on the journey that customers take with Cisco. Use of data to enhance employees' and partners' experience is at the center of this transformation. In the next chapter, I describe engagement platforms that are powered by this data in further detail. For example, in the interview referenced above, Martinez talks about using data to reduce the time it takes Cisco employees to go through the sales cycle.

Product usage data, commonly referred to as telemetry, can provide insights that Cisco's partners use to uncover new business opportunities. Information about how Cisco works with the partners is detailed on their website in a blog post titled "Reimagining Customer Experience: Seizing Our Opportunity Together, Today." This is important as Cisco sells and services its customers through a vast network of partners. So, it makes sense for Cisco to invest in data infrastructure which supports partners' success.

Imagine a scenario where customer-facing teams use a single dashboard that presents all the data we know about the customer. This dashboard would pull data from the CRM system about the products that customers recently bought and products that the customer is planning to buy. Then layer on pulling information from marketing systems to show who from the customer organization is engaging with our marketing content. The dashboard also includes data from post-sale teams—their interactions with the customer and their status.

This one-stop-shop for all this customer data can be used by the analytics team to build alerts based on certain triggers. For example, if the customer buys a product and does not implement it within a certain time frame, an alert is generated to the success team. If certain users are engaging with our marketing content, sales teams get an alert to follow-up with the customer as they could be ready to buy another product.

These are just some examples of how customer data is used at these companies, and I would argue that the use of customer data is in its early stages. Companies only combine data from a few places, most likely from CRM and marketing automation systems, and use it primarily as a tool to drive more sales. Data from post-sale interactions or interactions in other channels, like support sites and social media platforms, is not always used.

WHAT CAN BE DONE IN THE FUTURE

In a YouTube series called DigitalMinds on Cisco's channel, Steve Cox, a digital experience leader, talks about three things that we could do to realize the power of customer data. These three items paint a powerful vision for the future to which many organizations can aspire.

The first step is to collect all the data about the customer in one place to have a "360-degree view of the customer." Just collecting data is not enough. This data must be served to everyone in the company who engages with the customer, so they have the full context. The second step is to use the latest technologies, like artificial intelligence and machine learning, to recommend next steps to the users of this data. The amount of data can quickly get overwhelming to the users, leading to analysis paralysis. The purpose of data should be to drive more meaningful and valuable customer interactions. Lastly, we need to invest in digital platforms that various teams use to engage with the customer. We will talk more about these platforms in the next chapter.

Another powerful example of what a future with unified customer data can look like, is the vision for "care of one," as discussed in an article from McKinsey's website titled "The Vision for 2025: Hyperpersonalized Care and 'Care of One'." The authors describe a future where we will use all the information we have on a customer and provide a hyper-personalized customer service. In this future world, we will never need to contact a call center. Many of us will not miss listening to cheesy on-hold music when we call a service provider. In a B2B context, it goes beyond the annoyance of calling into a support line or logging into a website. If data can be used to identify problems before they happen, both vendors and customers can benefit from significant cost savings as a result.

To understand more about what this future can look like, imagine that customer feedback, behaviors, and trend data will flow directly from the contact center to the rest of the enterprise to improve products, marketing, or upstream interactions. The authors go on to say, "The 'care of one' model will be supported by advanced analytics, AI, real-time natural language processing, and other tools that detect customer sentiment and emotion. Cutting-edge agent-productivity tools will fully support the end-to-end interaction with automation for both the agent and the customer."

This future state described in these two scenarios is easy to imagine but hard to execute. Organizations will be wise to take a practical "crawl, walk, run" approach to gradually increasing their capabilities. The foundational capabilities discussed in earlier chapters are necessary to achieve this vision of collecting and using unified customer data. The authors in the McKinsey article on "care of one" cited above say, "Building a comprehensive customer profile requires a high level of cross-departmental visibility, which in turn necessitates enablers such as organizational structure changes and IT investments."

PITFALLS OF GETTING TO THE FUTURE STATE

It is not hard to get smart executives in any organization excited about ideas like "care of one" or "360-degree view of the customer." The challenge is to bring these ideas to life and put them into action. Even with the best of intentions, it is hard for new ideas to overcome organizational inertia. The first step is to have a senior leader in the organization be the champion and sponsor for the idea. We will talk more broadly about the role of different leaders in part three. For now, we will focus on the common pitfalls of implementing a unified customer data initiative.

As the famous saying goes, "How do you eat an elephant? One bite at a time." It is important to understand that building a unified view of the customer is a significant effort and multi-faceted problem. Starting small and getting quick wins will help show value and build the support needed over time. Look for obvious cases where data from more than one system can speed up someone's job. As an example, combine CRM data with product usage data to spot new sales opportunities. Combining support or service interaction data with sales opportunity data is another good use case. As we discussed earlier, most organizations combine sales and marketing data already, but product and post-sale data is often overlooked.

It is important to start with a list of questions that can be answered by the data. If the data is connected to someone's work, it creates an incentive to collect and maintain the data. Look no further than the questions that different departments are asking each other and look for areas where this data can help drive some sort of activity.

Do not limit yourself to only structured or quantitative data because qualitative and unstructured data, like the notes in a support ticket or meeting notes in a CRM system, can offer valuable insights; however, this type of data requires investment in more sophisticated, technical solutions, so they are not the first place to start. Using this type of data should be the long-term vision.

We are in the early stages of creating a unified view of the customer, especially in a B2B context. Advances in technology and examples from the B2C world offer opportunities to get started on this journey. More importantly, leaders in different roles realize that customer data offers a treasure trove of insights that can improve the effectiveness of their teams and provide a competitive advantage. Organizations will be wise to take a gradual, phased approach to collecting unified data.

CHAPTER 11

DIGITAL CUSTOMER ENGAGEMENT PLATFORM

When we think of Google Cloud's products, the first thing that comes to mind is the productivity suite with Gmail, Meet, Docs, etc. That is just the tip of the iceberg. A quick look through their website shows there is a myriad of products, like Looker—an analytics product, Apigee—an API management product, security products, and more. That is not even counting the more technical products, like server hosting, databases, and others. The point is that Google Cloud is a very complex ecosystem of products.

I interviewed Brian LaFaille, who joined Google through the acquisition of Looker and runs Customer Success Strategic Programs. Brian's work at Google is nothing like it was at Looker. At Looker, the customer base was more predictable, even with different sizes and complexity of companies. They had a playbook on how to run the CS business, starting with customer onboarding, CSM engagement, and the renewal process.

Brian told me that at Google, "Workspace [products like Gmail, Docs, etc.] has thirty-thousand customers, Looker has three thousand, Apigee has a thousand." The magnitude and scale of customers are very diverse—some of the customers are small companies and some are the world's largest, most complex organizations. He also said, "We have to be very careful in how we apply CSM resourcing and ensure that if a CSM is going to be on an account, they're going to drive meaningful impact on license utilization for that solution pillar."

Brian and his team found that the only way to scale customer success activities across this diverse customer base was to use a digital platform powered by the customer data. Being in a data-centric company, like Google, gives them a leg up as they can learn from their peers in the consumer side of the house.

The problem of scaling Customer Success is not unique to large companies like Google. Any company that has a lot of customers who need varied involvement from the vendor will have the same scale-related challenges. This challenge is not limited to internal team activities but can extend to customer interactions with the company.

Imagine the number of people, systems, and documents that a customer uses throughout their journey. Often, these systems are not designed with the customer in mind—think of support websites, presentations from sales and customer success teams, and emails and webinars from marketing. Imagine a system that gives employees access to all this data in one place, where they can track all their customer interactions. Better yet, the system can even recommend the right course of action using the customer data.

Imagine the customer experience we can create using the data we know about them. We can provide a one-stop-shop where the customer can track their progress toward value, recommend the right action, and surface the right type of resources to help. In other words, they are in charge of their own success journey.

That is the true north star for a digital platform—putting the customer in the driver's seat of success.

In this chapter, we will review the components of a digital platform, its uses by employees of the company and the customer, and what it takes to build a platform.

WHAT IS A DIGITAL PLATFORM?

In the previous chapter, we talked about the value of and use for customer data. Customer data by itself is not useful unless it is used to drive meaningful action. This action can be performed by an individual within the company, a collaboration between teams within the company, or between a vendor and the customer.

Let's look at common customer interactions. Customers may read an article about our products on a website, receive a call to action email asking them to do something like download a white paper or watch a webinar, meet with a salesperson to get a demo of the product, and use our products during a trial period. All these interactions take place before the customer starts paying for the product. After the initial sale, customer interactions are even more fragmented, using many different channels which range from the product itself to support websites, customer success teams, and so on.

The situation is not much better for employees within the company. Each team that interacts with the customer has their own set of tools, creating disparate data (discussed in the previous chapter). The wise old adage "It takes a village" is very much applicable to delivering great experiences and outcomes for customers. I'd add a variation to that: it takes a village full of people doing a whole lot of work to achieve customer success. It is not an easy endeavor to know what the right activity is, who is doing it, and where the hand offs are.

You get the picture. This is not a way to create great experiences. What we need is a single digital platform used by both the internal teams and our customers. But that is the north star, and it does not happen overnight.

Cisco, the technology giant, is creating a unified experience for all internal teams powered by data and using modern technologies like AI and ML. In a CX leader podcast, aptly titled "Bringing Down the Silos," Steve Cox, VP of digital lifecycle journeys at Cisco, says the "main thing I'm trying to do is drive an experience that connects all the way from market through renewal."

In the same podcast, Steve's colleague, Thimaya Subaiya, adds another critical piece of the puzzle: the organizational model. In other words, how work actually gets done and who does what in the process of getting the work done. He says, "Defining the role becomes the critical piece overall. The moment you back that up with a console, which is a technology based on interface, you are kind of forced to follow one singular process across the board. It could be here [in the US]. [It] could be in Asia. It could be in Europe. We're still following just one process. So, technology can help define the working methodology and the process that each one of these roles follow."

Cisco's example illustrates how a technology-enabled work process and a single "console" can deliver a great, consistent employee experience.

Sprinklr, the customer experience management platform, is solving for this problem by aggregating customer data from a number of sources like social media and messaging platforms. Sprinklr calls their platform a "unified customer experience platform," which is used by teams like marketing, advertising, and customer care with access to the same data about customers.

In both cases, these companies offer digital platforms powered by customer data to help internal teams do their jobs better, hopefully leading to better financial outcomes. These platforms are powered by the unified customer data (discussed in chapter ten) to proactively guide customers along in their journey. Customers get a cockpit of sorts to understand how they are using the products, the value they are getting, and where they are headed.

WHAT IS IT USED FOR?

The data that the company gathers from the customer, when presented in the right context, can empower the customer to be in control of their journey. This digital platform can be a powerful tool to put customers in the driver's seat of their success.

Imagine a scenario where the customer executive gets a 360-degree view of the status of their journey with data about products they are paying for, the status of implementation, the value they receive, and a recommended course of action. This is a dream-like scenario for both the customers and the vendors.

Telling internal teams to "work across silos" is not enough. They need tools and data to pinpoint where, how, and when to work across the silos. There is a similar analogy in other parts of a software company, particularly in the product development process. It is a common practice today to have self-contained, cross-functional teams using DevOps practices—indicating that development and operations teams are working together.

The same approach is needed when working with the customer. A digital platform, like the one that Cisco has built, can be a powerful enabler to promote cross-functional work. Customer data can be used to suggest the right course of action for each customer. This is similar to the "care of one" concept we discussed in Chapter ten.

WHAT ARE THE CHALLENGES AND PITFALLS OF BUILDING IT?

How do you know who you are designing the experience for? This is probably the biggest challenge because the scope of the answer to this question is enormous. The short answer is everyone, but that's not very useful.

Steve Cox describes it well in the podcast interview referenced earlier: "You need to engage the buyers, the sponsors, the executives, and the expectation of the customer. You tie these all together in a seamless experience." They focus not only on how to capture the data but also specific actions to take and who should take those actions. This helps Cisco teams to "engage those customers at the right time, with the right information, to the right person."

Building these processes and platforms is a long-term endeavor, which means it should be treated as a product that the company is building and continuously improving. Can you imagine a company building the product once and not investing in making changes? Of course not! In fact, it's the exact opposite of how product development works today. Just think of all the updates we receive on mobile apps.

A digital platform to engage customers and empower them on their customer success journey should be no different. This also means that there is an ongoing investment into this product. The payoffs on this investment will be well worth it. Better customer experience, increased customer retention, and better use of internal resources are just a few benefits from this investment.

CONCLUSION

As the number of customers grows and their profile becomes diverse, a digital platform is an essential element of customer success strategy. This platform will lead to a better experience for customers and employees. For the benefits of the platform to play out, it should be viewed as any other product we offer, with the right level of investment and management.

PART 3

WHAT CHANGES DO LEADERS NEED TO MAKE?

CHAPTER 12

CHIEF CUSTOMER OFFICER

Chief customer officers (CCOs) face an interesting paradox in their roles. "They are being asked to do two things that are hard by themselves and sometimes in conflict with each other. They are asked to contribute to revenue [through services, referrals, and customer growth] and be the standard bearer for the customer experience." This is what Charles Atkins, a partner at McKinsey & Company, who works with leading technology companies, told me in an interview.

Charles' observation presents an interesting and challenging opportunity for these leaders. A 2011 article in *Harvard Business Review* titled "The Rise of Chief Customer Officer" highlighted some of the challenges and opportunities. Even though the CCO role has been around for nearly a decade and has become more common recently, it is not common to see CCOs focus on the revenue goal. The article states, "It's not just about fixing problems—it's about accelerating growth" and expresses a worry that "we will see lots of flameouts." We are not past these challenges as the CCO role, and the scope of responsibility continues to change. While the worry about "flameouts" has not panned out, we are far from having a standard definition of the CCO role.

Most CS teams are hyper-focused on processes to help customers in the post-sale portion of the customer journey, which directly affects retention revenue and services revenue. It is more common for CCOs to own not just Customer Success teams but also have Professional Services and Support reporting to them. As we discussed in chapter six, some of the services needed in the post-sale customer journey are covered in this org structure.

The harder mandate to fulfill is to be the standard bearer for the customer as it involves getting all go-to-market peers aligned on the customer context. This goes back to the first part of the model we discussed earlier in the book. Do all the c-suite have a common understanding of customers and their motivations? Do all these teams speak the same language? Achieving this alignment is no easy task, especially while building a new revenue generating function.

Even though most companies say customer success is a priority, no one from the senior leadership really "owns" this priority. This is where CCOs can step in and take charge.

This is not an easy path forward. In many cases, CCOs will have to do the "championing" through influence; in other words, they won't have the explicit authority to drive change. That is understandable because the change we need will upset the "ways of working" of other departments, which are led by peers of the CCO.

Navigating the executive suite and nudging their peers toward a customer success mindset is the biggest challenge. Another equally challenging aspect of the CCO role is to build organizational capabilities—which includes people, process, and technology changes—that support these two mandates.

PEOPLE

In Chapter eight, we discussed frameworks to package the right set of services and channels to deliver customer success. Hiring the right set of skills is more challenging for a CCO than any of their peer executives. The skill set needs change as the product and the company matures, so CCOs will find themselves in a constant hiring mode.

The common thread in hiring across different roles is what I call, "customer-in thinking." It is important that anyone that a CCO hires has a deep understanding of and empathy for customer needs. This is not a very hard skill to test for in the interviews. The standard behavioral questions can help test for a candidate's approach to problem-solving. The test is, "Do they approach solutions starting with the customer in mind?"

Additionally, given the diverse nature of teams that a CCO is responsible for, it is imperative they hire strong leaders who can build these teams. It is not enough to decide the right set of services needed and hire the right leaders; it is equally important to determine the right organization structure and incentives. For example, if the teams are structured by the type of services they offer—project-based, relationship-based, etc.—how would they work in tandem to deliver the right outcomes to the customer? Alternately, if they are organized by customer segments like industry, the challenge is to have consistent practices across teams.

One of the emerging needs I noted in my research is the need for better collaboration between post-sale teams and product teams. I heard it from leaders of both these teams as they realized that post-sale services teams are best positioned to be the "eyes and ears" for the product team. Product teams can benefit from learning how customers are using the product in real life and the challenges they face.

When I was leading Customer Success at Gartner, I would spend a great deal of time with the product leader, sharing my team's experience from the field and getting his help for challenging customer situations. This was easy for us as we were a small team, but it can become more challenging with larger organizations. Services teams need to think about effective ways to communicate this information to the product teams without making it too complicated.

I have seen a simple solution work where both teams make it part of at least one person's job to be the liaison to the other team. Customer Success may hire someone with product management skills and make them responsible for gathering and summarizing product-related feedback.

One not so radical approach could be to have some sort of rotation program between services and product teams, where certain members will be "visiting staff" on the other teams.

PROCESS

Post-sale teams must serve different types of customers (as discussed in chapters four through six of the model) and do so using a wide range of services (as discussed in chapters seven through nine of the model). Putting all these different puzzle pieces together is the biggest challenge on the horizon for CCOs.

One approach that works is to start with a prescriptive list of outcomes that the company's offerings support. This is detailed in chapter six. Even before this language is adopted by other functions, it will help service teams to focus on specific outcomes. CCOs should expect their teams to develop standard processes—onboarding, implementation, training, etc.—around these outcomes. Then they should educate other functions on their approach so there are clear expectations on customer engagement activities in the post-sale portion of the journey. That will inevitably lead to two things: first, it will prompt a dialogue on any differences in how we talk about value with our customers, and second, sales teams will see the value in including post-sale teams during the sales process.

CCOs can also use their influence with their peer executives to change "on the ground" processes (as discussed in chapter eight) to increase collaboration between different functions. Ideally, they can change incentive structures, but that might be a harder sell as sales and marketing leaders will be hesitant to change what is, in their view, working.

TECHNOLOGY

Every other customer-facing function has a mature set of technologies, but given the disparate set of functions that a CCO manages, there is no one technology solution that is suited for the "customer" function. There are customer success solutions for customer success teams, professional services automation solutions to manage resources in a project-based services org, solutions to track support tickets, learning management systems, and so on.

One of the big investments that a CCO can target is consolidating all customer data together and using this data to trigger action, at first by their own teams. Once they prove the value of using customer data, they can explore valuable use cases for sales and marketing teams.

Shreesha Ramdas, founder of Strikedeck, told me in an interview that Customer Success—which I interpret to mean the CCOs organization—can be the "custodian of customer data." This org can not only collect all the data but also provide this data to different functions across the company. Many CCOs I interviewed are starting to realize that their knowledge of the customer context can be the lever they need to influence the changes in other functions.

Being the owner of customer data is a valuable role for the CCO to play. This helps them fulfil the second mandate we discussed at the beginning of the chapter—be the steward of the customer or internal customer champion.

LOOKING AHEAD

The CCO has an important role to play in making customer success a common thread across different functions. They can lead the charge in shifting the internal operating model from that of managing customer transactions to managing the entire customer journey. CCOs must push changes internally to hire differently, advocate for process changes, and invest in technology to become the customer champion.

How will the role of CCO change over the next three to five years?

In response to their revenue responsibilities, CCOs will build "shadow" sales and marketing organizations within their functions. One of the widely debated questions among CS leaders is "Should CS carry a revenue target?" The short answer is yes. The answer is more nuanced if the question becomes "Should CS teams be compensated like sales teams on a commission basis?" If a significant portion of the revenue comes from existing customers, and CCOs are accountable for this revenue, they will need sales and marketing skills within their departments.

CCOs will need to build capabilities within their organizations to adequately fulfill their role of growing revenues from existing customers. One such opportunity for change is in building marketing teams under CCOs. As marketing functions change to support the entire customer journey, a lot of their priorities are informed by post-sale teams. In the current organization models, marketing has an affinity to "serve" sales, and the best way to break that mold is housing a marketing function under the CCO.

CCOs will need to stand up parallel product development capabilities in cases where the product offerings are complex technical solutions. Customer needs from such solutions are always one step ahead of the product teams' ability to deliver. Post-sale teams, particularly professional services teams, can play a big role in plugging the gaps in the product feature set. One way to do this is hiring product development and engineering skills, where the development activity and resulting knowledge do not happen in isolation. Rather these teams become an extension of product teams co-creating features.

The technology stack to support customer success is fragmented, and the solutions available today are immature. In response, CCOs will own the biggest technology budget of all functions in the company. This is especially true in larger companies, but CCOs at all companies will be forced to build their own technology solutions.

The bottom line is that the title of the article "The Rise of Chief Customer Officer" is even more relevant today than it was in 2011.

CHAPTER 13

CHIEF SALES OFFICER

Christian Conti, who knows a thing or two about sales in a subscription business because he has spent twenty plus years managing sales teams in such a business. When I asked him, "What should the sales teams do to increase chances of renewal?" he replied, "I'll tell you what they shouldn't do. Deals done by reps who are lone wolves are always risky. The smaller the number of fingerprints on a deal, the less healthy the deal is in the longer term."

His take on a good deal is when there are "many fingerprints on the deal." He wants and values different perspectives—sales, product, services—on the best solution for the customer.

Good sales leaders know that customer success starts with them. In a talk at a TSIA conference titled "Aligning Sales, Services, and Marketing Around Customer Success," former chief revenue officer of HubSpot Mark Roberge said that customers want "helpful, intelligent, and prescriptive individuals" as their salespeople. He ended the talk by asking, "Is the future of sales ... services?"

What do these leaders know and do that other sales leaders can learn from? In this chapter, we will review the implications of the new customer success model on sales teams and what sales leaders can do to help their teams be part of this model.

PEOPLE

Starting with the basics, look at the onboarding and training programs to see how much time is spent on teaching about customer personas, their motivations for buying the product, and the customer's definition of value. It is worth looking at the time and effort spent on gaining product knowledge *vs.* building customer empathy. Value realization models, discussed in chapter six, are great source material for sales training.

This is not to diminish product training but to reorient product training to look at products as solutions to customer problems, not just cool widgets. More importantly, invest in teaching sales teams about the motivations of the customers and the jobs the customers are trying to do. Do the sales teams understand customers' jobs to be done and how the company's service offerings support the customers' entire journey? Sales teams must understand all services available to the customers. A good rule of thumb that I like, and many in the Customer Success field propose, is to have a slide on post-sale services in the first call deck.

My team at ServiceNow publishes best practices that customers should follow to accelerate their journey toward value. We provide step-by-step guidance on different activities that customers should undertake to set the right foundations, implement the right products, manage the ServiceNow platform, and grow customer teams' skills and capabilities. This content gives our teams credibility and gives our customers confidence that we are bringing the right expertise to the table. Not surprisingly, our sales teams and customers love this content.

Sales teams need help in the form of the right messaging and content they can use in the sales process. Applying the same level of rigor to training sales teams on post-sale services will give the sales teams confidence in setting the right expectations with the customers.

Emilia D'Anzica, Founder of GrowthMolecules, a Customer Success consulting company, wrote a blog post titled "How to Fix Sales & Success Friction" on the 'nuffsaid website, which features many interesting pieces on customer success. In this article, Emilia says, "It's no secret: the Sales and Customer Success partnership is easy to botch." She goes on to list several areas of friction between Sales and Customer Success.

Some of the friction points are lack of alignment on product use cases, lack of understanding of what it takes to onboard customers, miscommunication on access to success resources, and missing information about contacts needed by CS teams (remember our section on buyer-implementer-user from chapter four). Many of these frictions point to one root cause: lack of alignment and common understanding of customers, success as defined by the customer, and what it takes to make customers successful.

Post-sale teams have access to a lot of customer data that can be very useful to coach sales teams. Customer Success teams, for example, use data to define profiles of successful customers by correlating customer characteristics and product usage to renewal outcomes. This data can be used in the sales cycle to qualify customers and guide them toward the best fit usage of the product.

These are just three different ways sales teams can change their training and skills development programs. In the same talk referenced above, Roberge talks about an analysis that showed them that the variation in renewal performance can be traced back to sales reps. They used this data to change the sales compensation structure but could very well have used this data to coach individual reps (note: they may well have done this, but it was not covered in that talk).

PROCESS

Nearly all Customer Success leaders I interviewed mentioned that getting involved in the sales process is a good practice to help customers realize value. Most of them talked about coaxing the sales leaders or using personal relationships as leverage to make it happen. In other words, sales and success teams working together still does not happen by design. This is a missed opportunity for both teams and, more importantly, for the customers.

I often think about my time leading the Customer Success team at CEB. We had a sales rep in Australia who was selling this product like it was hotcakes. He exceeded his goals and everyone's expectations and sold twice as much as his given quota. We even had to hire a dedicated customer success manager to support our customers in Australia. While serving all these customers, we realized most of these deals did not have many fingerprints, as Conti put it. This sales rep in Australia was a lone wolf.

Anyone who must manage the renewal side of a business needs to make sure that, in Christian's words, "There are many fingerprints on a deal." In the next generation of customer success, work processes should be designed to include this collaboration, supported by changes to the incentives and processes as discussed in chapter nine.

"Don't let implementation come in the way of a sale" is a common mindset among sales teams, who worry that talking about implementation in the sales process will slow them down or, worse, derail the deal. That is short-sighted thinking. Customers buy into the promise of value in the sales process and expect to realize this vision. A well-defined post-sale process can set the vendors apart.

TECHNOLOGY

We have already discussed how important customer data is to achieve customer success. Customer data offered in an easy to access and use system, with the right context, is the dream material for good sales teams. The challenge is to identify the right customer data and insights that help bring in more leads and close deals faster. CRM systems are not often designed to collect customer data, and systems in the post-sale processes are not used by the sales teams.

This brings us to the story we discussed in chapter ten about how Aaron Fulkerson created a customer database at ServiceNow. He made this data available to everyone and created an incentive for different teams not only to use but also to contribute data. This virtuous cycle created a valuable data source and system that helps all the teams. Sales leaders can then take a more active role to invest in systems that capture customer data as well.

Customer data by itself is not sufficient without applying it in the right context, an effort to which both sales and post-sale teams can contribute, and context has never been more important than in 2020 amidst the global pandemic. To illustrate the importance of context, let's look at how Gartner measures consumption.

Each Gartner customer gets access to a variety of services: access to analyst reports, attendance at webinars, discussion with an expert on a given topic, access to data tools, a certain number of in-person workshops, etc. In my interview with Christian, he told me that in 2020, they noticed the number of services customers were consuming on average had increased, from 4.2 in the prior year to 4.4 on a scale that ranges from one to five. This would have the service team believe they are doing a better job and expect to see an increase in renewals.

What is lost in these numbers is that customers were consuming certain types of services more than others; for example, they were reading more analyst reports. After all, we all found ourselves with extra time when most social activity was curtailed. Christian and his team know that customers value in-person workshops higher than other services, and travel restrictions, along with other distractions, have made it harder to conduct in-person workshops.

This type of insight can only come to light when different teams work together and add their own knowledge and context to the data. Sales teams have a big role to play in contributing to the contextual data they learn from their interactions with customers.

LOOKING AHEAD

In this chapter, we reviewed different people, process, and technology changes that sales leaders can implement in the new customer success model. Some of these changes, like a sales process that includes CS teams, are the easiest to implement, whereas changes around skills sets and data take longer to implement. Overall, these changes are mostly incremental to how sales teams are organized and operate.

What would some more drastic changes to the Sales function look like?

The new model of customer success will challenge our conventional understanding of sales and customer success. The boundary between these functions might become blurry. It would not be surprising to see customer success leaders become sales leaders. We will see new organizational structures that don't conform to the traditional structures with which we are familiar.

As revenue growth comes from expanding customer spending, sales leaders need to be skilled at managing the entire customer journey. In emerging business models, like product-led growth and usage-based pricing, the way we organize teams will see more pod-like teams led by general managers, consisting of sales, marketing, and customer success professionals. We saw a glimpse of it in the HubSpot example quoted above.

The skills profiles of sales leaders are another possible place we may see a change. If a deep understanding of customers is a prerequisite in the new customer success model, we will see more customers joining the vendors in sales roles. It is common to see customers join CS or professional services, and it may not be a stretch to see customers join sales roles.

CHAPTER 14

CHIEF MARKETING OFFICER

Marketing is about telling stories that inspire customers to act. Stated more simply, marketing convinces customers to buy the products we make. Yes, I know, marketing does a lot more than that, but that's the gist of it.

In the SaaS world, aren't all customers making buying decisions? Isn't a renewal a buying decision? Does marketing have a role in this? Why would marketing stop the story midway at the end of the sales process?

When I talked to Allyn Horne, who has led product marketing for several tech businesses, including Amazon and Rocket Fuel, he agreed that marketing plays a critical role not only in customer acquisition but also in engagement and retention. In fact, many marketing departments align teams around customer lifecycle stages to support the customer even beyond purchase.

In a blog post titled "The Evolution of Customer Lifecycle" on marketing automation software Marketo's site, "purchase" is the third out of six stages in the lifecycle. It is worth noting that the customer lifecycle is divided equally between the pre-sales and post-sales processes in a number of steps. Of course, marketing's role is slightly different across the customer lifecycle—in the sales process, marketing is focused on generating demand by painting the vision of value, whereas post-sales, the need is to educate, encourage, and inspire customers to use our products and turn customers into advocates for our products and brand.

Turning customers into avid fans, advocates, and growth drivers is not just marketing's job. While every other customer-facing team has a role, the focus of this chapter is on changes to marketing's role in the customer success model. Marketing leaders must reimagine their role and make deliberate changes across people, process, and technology areas, and in this chapter, we will review some of the recommended changes.

PEOPLE

In the reimagined Customer Success model, we expand the definition of customer as discussed in chapter four. We discussed that "buyers" are no longer the only customers; implementers and users are customers as well. Even the customer's customer should be considered a customer.

This expanded view of customers means marketers have a much broader audience for their messaging than they did previously. Marketers need to have empathy for different types of customers and communicate effectively with all of them in all stages of their journey. This changes the profile of a typical marketing hire as they need to be able to write content that offers insights into the entire journey, from the awareness stage to implementation and renewal.

On the people front, one common question is about reporting structure—should customer marketing report to the customer success team or the marketing team? In my opinion, there is no right answer. Marketing teams have processes built in that can be used for both demand generation activities and customer marketing activities. In that sense, having all of marketing under one department provides the advantage of using scalable processes. The intimate knowledge of customers is a factor that would favor having a marketing team within customer success.

Marketing leaders need to cast a wider net for candidates with skill sets and experience in consulting and research. Besides having good customer-first thinking, these candidates bring deeper data analysis skills, which are critical for marketing teams. At ServiceNow, my team is responsible for writing best practices on what it takes to implement and manage the ServiceNow platform. Even though we are not marketers, our content is used by marketing teams in their customer communications. This content is also used by Customer Success teams to help customers in implementation initiatives.

PROCESS

The conventional purpose of the Marketing machine, if we can call it that, is to attract prospective customers to the company's products and services. It is to generate interest in the promise we are making and convince future customers that it is relevant to their lives. Increasingly, Marketing needs to focus not just on attracting new customers but on increasing the "wallet share," of existing customers, a measure of higher spending by customers. One of the metrics for marketing teams is the number of sales leads they generate, but in the new model, teams should measure customer retention and loyalty.

In the early stages of the customer journey, Marketing's role is to paint a vision for the customer, and in later stages after the purchase, Marketing's role is to give the customer confidence that they are on the path to success. What type of marketing efforts will help drive that confidence? How would we measure success?

Let us take demand generation activity, like a webinar or a blog post. In the early stages, the goal is to get customer information and maybe an idea about their intent to buy. For a customer in the onboarding stage, the purpose of the webinar or other type of content is to increase product usage and get the customer closer to success. It is harder to measure the specific action that a customer takes.

Marketing can play an important role in onboarding new customers, especially for less complicated products or for less complex tasks. In chapter five, we discussed how Stephen Horning's customer success team at Pantheon defined a maturity model for WebOps. This content is valuable for customers to assess their practices against a standard model and define a path to improving their practices. This type of content is typically created by post-sale customer success teams, but it can be very helpful for marketing teams to launch onboarding campaigns for new customers. This gives the customers confidence that the company has what it takes to fulfill the promises.

As the focus shifts to the entire customer lifecycle, marketing departments will increasingly align with customer lifecycle stages and audiences, enabling marketers to create thoughtful leadership content tailored to the specific business contexts of those audiences. This content aims not only to inspire customers but also to provide clear guidance and answers to the "how to" questions of customers.

To support CS teams in helping new customers experience immediate value from products, Allyn's teams created onboarding playbooks. These playbooks contained not only audience-relevant product information and positioning but also detailed case studies that illustrated the timing and sequence of products that customers adopted to gain maximum value for their products. These case studies were rooted in adoption curves, jointly defined by marketing and product teams, that highlighted the optimal use of products to balance customer needs and customer lifetime value.

In an ad tech context, Allyn describes how an advertiser new to running digital ads might maximize ROAS (return on ad spend) by beginning their digital media campaigns with display ads. As they gain comfort with digital marketing, the advertiser may add instream or outstream video ad placements (ads that run at the beginning, middle, or end of online videos). Later, they might pursue over the top (OTT) video ads (think of the ads we see while watching Hulu or Amazon Prime) and audio ads. How can we nudge customers along this path? Allyn sees this as a critical role for marketing. After all, a good marketer can tell a story and convince customers to act.

The marketing process is built to support one-to-many communications, and onboarding processes are a good fit for this mode of communication. This requires that the Marketing team have an ongoing process that ties their activities with those of Customer Success teams. In this case, Marketing teams will be providing visibility into the "health" of the customer pipeline instead of the prospect pipeline.

At ServiceNow, one of the most popular programs our Customer Marketing team runs is digital onboarding. All new customers get a series of emails that guide them through specific steps they should take. These steps include registering for the community site, attending training courses, watching product implementation videos, and more.

Marketing and Customer Success, or any other post-sales services teams, should work on a clear definition of roles and responsibilities for customer interactions and events in the lifecycle. Define specific activities within the journey and assign ownership for each team. For example, CS can own creating the onboarding content while Marketing owns distributing it in various channels, like emails or community blog posts. Marketing should own tracking what customers are doing with the content, but CS should own follow-up.

These are a few examples of how existing marketing processes can be used or modified for post-sale activities.

TECHNOLOGY

Anyone who has worked in or with Marketing teams realizes that Marketing is a very data-heavy function. Behind the scenes of glossy images and catchy slogans, there is typically a big data operation that analyzes everything about a user—whether they clicked on a link or downloaded a document. Marketing can even analyze the user's IP address to identify the company the user works for.

We know that Marketing teams are very good at using customer data in a consumer context, and the same techniques can be applied in an enterprise context. Marketing teams can be big consumers of and contributors to customer data. They can bring their data analytics prowess to helping customers adopt products better and get value faster. Marketing teams can also use customer data to automate customer success processes, like onboarding, expanding product usage, and realizing and communicating value.

Allyn told me that, while leading product marketing at Rocket Fuel, he and his team partnered with the product team to identify a series of high-value actions that customers could take after onboarding. For example, they realized that the best time for customers to manually review and adjust budgets was between seven and fourteen days after initial set up. So, they worked with the product team to code alerts in the software and emails to prompt customers to review their budgets after five days, with alerts also delivered to customer success teams.

This is not easy. According to Allyn, "There is always a tension between implementing change to tell the full story *vs.* running demand generation." With the right data on revenue retention and allowing CS teams to focus on higher value tasks, there is a way to do it.

LOOKING AHEAD

In the new Customer Success model, Marketing teams will need to expand the types of skills and backgrounds they hire to better support customers throughout their lifecycle. They will be able to use or need to change the marketing processes to support the goals of the post-sale stages of the customer lifecycle. This requires a clear definition of roles across Marketing and other teams—essentially "Who does what and when?" with customers.

Looking out three to five years, what changes can we expect?

Customer data is already central to Marketing teams' strategy and operations, and it is only bound to increase. Marketing teams can play a big role in defining how we handle unified customer data, an element of the customer success model we discussed in chapter ten. Marketing already has initiatives, like account-based marketing, and these efforts will get a boost from more unified customer data. Marketing will become the biggest consumer of product usage data and the resulting insights into customer needs.

This increased use of data will put Marketing in a position to facilitate the go-to-market strategy that is focused on the entire customer journey. This begins with the right content frameworks that start with a deep understanding of the customer. Content creation has always been a core part of Marketing's role, but Marketing teams can play a bigger role outside of their functional silo. Marketing and Customer Success can partner to create content frameworks to enable a cross-functional view of the customer.

In the chapter on chief customer officers, I mentioned that CCOs will need to stand up their own sales and marketing functions as they are accountable for a major portion of company revenue. Central Marketing teams, managed by the CMO, will take on a consultative role to other marketing functions instead of growing their own teams. They will set up centers of excellence to provide shared offerings, such as consistent content frameworks, marketing automation, and operations support.

The new model for customer success presents an opportunity to reimagine the role of marketing in advancing the growth of the company.

CHAPTER 15

CHIEF PRODUCT OFFICER

I was talking to one of my product manager friends about my book and the first element of the model, "Define your customer." His immediate reaction was, "We've got it. We know who our customers are." What he was saying was that defining the customer is not a problem for his company.

I then asked, "What does your CS team say is one of the reasons for churn?"

"Oh, they say we sell to the wrong customer," he answered.

"But I thought you said you guys knew who your customers were," I replied.

It is a bit of a paradox, isn't it? If they know who their customers are, how come they are selling to the wrong customer and failing to keep the customers long-term? I have had a similar conversation with many product managers, and I got many versions of the same "Oh, we've got that under control" answer. What I find interesting is the confidence they have when they answer the question, "Do you know your customers?" It's also interesting how little time they want to spend talking about it. Ask them about the cool new feature they are building instead, and they'll talk about it for hours.

I understand. They love building and releasing new products and features and get most excited about the next cool feature using the latest technology out there. Product managers, at heart, are problem solvers. They just need to focus on the problem of product adoption and customer value.

In this chapter, we will discuss what changes chief product officers (CPOs) can make to instill a customer success mindset in their teams. This will require changes in the team skill set as well as process and technology changes to encourage the mindset.

PEOPLE

The common approach product managers take to "understand their customers" is building personas. A persona is typically a person performing a specific role, say as a project manager or a salesperson. Then, they design products to help this persona with specific activities, or more simply put, helping them do their job better. What gets lost in this approach is the human element of the persona. Why are they using our product? What emotions do they experience as they use the product? How does the use of the product fit into their context and their motivations?

It is the responsibility of the product leader to build a team that has great empathy for their users. This will take more than training the team on techniques like design thinking. Product managers should understand customers' jobs to be done and build products focused on making it easy to complete the entire job.

Brightfield is a data analytics company that helps organizations with their extended workforce—anyone who is not an employee, like contractors and consultants. A big step in implementing their solution involves collecting massive amounts of data from customers' systems. The product team at Brightfield helps customers with this phase of implementation, in essence doing the work that a post-sale services team would do. This experience offers the product team insights into the common challenges and opportunities to make the data collection process easier, faster, and cheaper. This, in turn, leads to delivering customer value faster.

Stephen Horning, who I introduced in an earlier chapter, runs a Customer Success team at Pantheon, a web hosting company. The product team at Pantheon created a dedicated product manager role who works with CS and other customer-facing teams to serve as the eyes and ears for the product team. Stephen designated a member of his team to be the "liaison" to the product team to streamline the feedback into the product team.

These are two examples of team and people changes to foster product and CS team collaboration. The goal here is to help the product team learn how customers are using the products, challenges in implementing the product, and building customer empathy, as we discussed earlier.

PROCESS

One of the common reasons companies realize the need for Customer Success is to fill the gaps in product features. No matter the size and stage of the company, there is a gap in what the product is capable of doing and what customers expect from the product. This is natural and healthy for the product to continue to grow. In their book, *The Customer Success Economy*, Nick Mehta and Allison Pickens call this role of customer success the "CSM of the Gaps."

Besides helping the customers meet their needs, this "CSM of the Gaps" role is one of the best sources for ideas for new features. Product leaders need a process to gather these ideas and get additional context about the customer needs. They need to know whether the gaps in product features are consistent across multiple customers or if they only exist for a handful of customers. Then they can analyze these gaps from a cost-benefit standpoint.

It is not uncommon for product teams to lack a formal process for hearing valuable customer feedback. Product leaders should work with their counterparts to build "listening posts" where their teams can hear and learn from other customer-facing teams.

Collecting product usage data is a common technique used by product teams to understand how customers are using the product. This data can offer valuable insight into customer retention and expansion. Most people know the famous example in which Slack's product team knew that users who have sent two thousand messages are much more likely to continue using the product.

Product usage data can be overwhelming in its volume, and finding the magic number, like Slack did, is like finding a needle in a haystack. Sometimes, product usage data can be misleading when there is a gap between expected usage and actual usage of the product. It is imperative to look at this data in the context of other information about the customer, like change in stakeholders, having a clear vision and direction for the product.

Product leaders should put processes in place to analyze product usage data with input from other teams, like customer success, professional services, and sales.

TECHNOLOGY

Customer Success teams have the challenge of scaling their capacity across the customer segments. Many customer-facing teams try to solve the scale challenge by developing value stories and metrics as we discussed in chapter ten, in which we looked at two examples from Sprinklr and WalkMe.

The best solution to scale success across all customers is to build products with customer success in mind. Imagine a scenario where the product has features that guide customers through a recommended path of usage. This will eliminate the need for post-sale teams to work with customers on low-value, easy-to-automate tasks during product implementation and ongoing usage. Rather, these teams can focus their time on more complex customers.

In fact, in my interviews with leaders at companies, like Asha Aravindakshan of Sprinklr and Stephen Horning of Pantheon, I learned that these companies are trying to implement nudges within the product to guide the customers through different use cases. This approach is even more relevant and, in fact, critical to product-led growth companies (e.g., Zoom, Canva) where the product is the engine for sales and success. In these cases, customers start using a free version of the product and pay to use advanced features, with very little to no interaction with a Sales team.

Once we know what successful usage of the product looks like, it is easy to show the value being realized to the customer. This may not be easy right from the beginning, but that aspiration will drive product teams to design features that help customers use and see value, not just features that attract new customers.

These types of changes will require support from the product leader, who is responsible for resource allocation decisions.

Product features are, no doubt, the key factor in delivering value to the customer. By building teams that have greater customer empathy and supporting them with the right process and technology investments, product leaders can play a significant role in delivering customer success.

LOOKING AHEAD

Generating insights from product usage data to understand how and where customers are in their journey is common today. Product leaders have a big role in generating these insights. In the future, product leaders need to invest in putting this data in the right context. Product teams can play a role in creating a unified view of the customer by combining data from other functions, like Marketing, Sales, and Support. This combined data will be used to create customized experiences in the product.

As customer needs stay one step ahead of product functionality; product teams will fund professional services or customer success teams that work closely with the engineering teams in early implementations. By working directly with customers, product teams can better prioritize their investments.

The career paths for product and customer success teams will intertwine, with CS professionals becoming product managers and vice versa. This will lead to better products based on solving challenges for different types of customers. In the new model, product teams will be at the forefront of delivering customer success.

CHAPTER 16

CONCLUSION

What's next for Customer Success? That's the question I wanted to answer when I started writing this book. Having spent nearly ten years in Customer Success, I wanted to learn where the profession is headed and what companies should do differently to help customers succeed.

What I found is that customer success as we know it today is not what it will be or should be in the future. There are two common ways we understand customer success today: one, it is a post-sale function that companies create to manage customer relationships, and two, customer success is a business imperative. I realized early on that disproportionate effort is focused on the "customer success as a function" aspect.

While there is near universal agreement that customer success is a business imperative, it often seems like we are paying lip service. Each of today's leaders needs an approach to make customer success an essential part of organizing the entire company's operations.

My goal with this book is to change the conversation of customer success as an organizing principle for the entire company. I wanted to provide a framework that technology company leaders can use to reimagine their operations—where everything starts and ends with the success of the customer.

I detailed this problem with current thinking and proposed a new model for customer success in the first part of the book. In the second part, I described how the eight elements of the new model come to life using a range of stories and ideas.

Customer Success started as a post-sale function in response to the software as a service business model, where retaining customers and convincing customers to spend more are central to the growth of a software company. However, the state of customer success today is filled with confusion and complexity, which is only made worse by emerging business models, like product-led growth and usage-based pricing models. Thinking of Customer Success as one of the functions within the company is limiting and promotes siloed thinking.

To break down the silos, companies need to start unifying all teams' understandings of the customer context. We need to understand those who are involved in using our products and services, starting with the executive sponsors to the end users. Each of these people has a different motivation and definition of success as they interact with our product. Frameworks like jobs to be done can help us understand the true motivations of our customers at functional and emotional levels. Companies that realize that value is defined by these customers have different elements invested in developing a common language that all customer-facing teams use among themselves and with customers.

Within the company context, customer success should be thought of as a portfolio of services, not just a function. Depending on customer context and what they expect of the company, this portfolio of services can be packaged differently and delivered across different channels. This portfolio of services and how they are delivered changes as the company and customer contexts change. Lastly, we need to change incentives and work processes to support the "Customer success is everyone's job." mindset.

Some of the leading companies are looking at collecting and using all customer data available to us. This data can be used to create great experiences for employees and customers. Employees across the different functions can work together on a single platform that provides insights from the customer data and prompts the right activity. Similarly, data can power a new way to engage customers, providing personalized guidance on their journey with our company.

In my view, the reimagined world of customer success will change how all customer-facing functions work. We need to rethink who we hire, what skills are important, how we train the employees, and how work gets done across functions. The leaders of different functions need to step up and drive some of these changes. These leaders cannot be anchored to the current understandings of these roles. My hope is that we will all come at these changes with an open mind and with the success of the customer as the common end goal we are working toward.

My hope for anyone who reads through this book is that you take specific actions to work across silos to make customer success part of everyone's job. I hope you will be inspired by the principles, ideas, and stories in this book to make these changes. Finally, I hope this book adds to the conversation around customer success and helps us reimagine how customer success drives the organization of the future.

ACKNOWLEDGEMENTS

Whoever came up with the phrase "It takes a village" must have been an author. So many people were with me throughout this journey. Some helped me think, some helped me write, some offered support and encouragement, and many were just there. Thank you!

First and foremost, thank you to my family and friends for your unwavering support, and especially for the constant encouragement throughout this book writing journey. Special thanks to my wife, Hana, for constant encouragement and giving me the time and space I needed to write. To my boys, Daniel Anish and Adam-Lohit, thank you for your unflinching belief in me and for being the best cheerleaders that I could hope for. To my parents, thank you for laying the foundation of a learning and growth mindset from the beginning. And to my friends—Aleem, Animesh, Bilal, Charan, Dilip, Jim, and Venu—thank you for being in my corner no matter what.

I would also like to thank Eric Koester and everyone at Creator Institute for making book writing accessible. I could not have written the book without the amazing program, a movement, you have built. Thank you to the amazing team at New Degree Press (NDP) who have helped every step of the way, especially Rachel Mensch and Michelle Pollack for your editing support, John Saunders for being a great sounding board whenever I needed help, and Brian Bies for running a well-oiled machine.

Who knew writing a book was actually a community activity? I could not have gone through all it takes to write a book without the support of the wonderful group of fellow authors I met in the program, so thank you Asha, Ester, Ethan, Komal, and Mohamad for your friendship, support, and late-night writing sessions. You all have made this journey much more enjoyable.

My interest in new ideas and writing them down started with my time at CEB. To everyone I came across at CEB, thank you for the inspiration. Special thanks to many friends and mentors who I met at CEB who played a role in my book journey and helped to push my thinking: Allyn Horne, Brian Foster, Christian Conti, Chandramouli (CM), Haniel Lynn, Kavitha Venkita, Mark Tonsetic, and Todd Burner.

One of the benefits of writing this book was learning from the amazing community of leaders who are equally passionate about this topic. Thank you to everyone who spoke to me and allowed me to tell your stories. Aaron Fulkerson, Allyn Horne, Aron Kuehnemann, Asha Aravindakshan, Ashvin Vaidyanathan, Brian La Faille, Brian Foster, Bryan Prout, Charles Atkins, Charles Williams, Christian Conti, Chandramouli (CM), Dean Robison, Emilia D'Anzica, Faisal Raza,

Irit Eizips, Jamey Jeff, Jason Noble, Jason Whitehead, Jennifer Chiang, Liz Gilliam, Marty Kaufman, Niranjan Karhade, Nora Khalili, Ragy Thomas, Rav Dhaliwal, Rick Wright, Sam Loveland, Shreesha Ramdas, Stephen Horning, Todd Burner, Todd Eby, and UVL Narayana.

Finally, thank you to everyone who supported my pre-sales campaign. Without your generosity, it would not have been possible to bring this book to life. To Alex Khayo, Animesh Mathur, Doug Pitek, Haniel Lynn, Jamie Dorner, Jim Luetkemeyer, Justin Catchings, Karen Cangialosi, Karen Werner, Mark Tonsetic, Marty Kaufman, Michael Murphy, Paul Nicknig, Prabhakar Goriparthi, Raj Kovuru, Rob Pickering, Sze-Kei Jordan, and Todd Burner, special thanks for being top contributors to my campaign. For all those who supported my book in any way they could, thank you for your support and backing; you helped make the publishing of this book possible!

Aaron Fulkerson
Abhimanyu Raina
Abhinav Srivastava
Ahmed Jamal Bouaichi
Aleem Meerapuram
Alex Khayo
Allyn Horne
Amarendra Kondapalli
Andrew Beales
Andrew Shanks
Andy Udell
Animesh Mathur
Anjali Joshi
Ankush Agarwal
Ann Eilers
Anoo Roche
Anthony Donatelli
Arash Hazer
Aron Kuehnemann
Asha Aravindakshan
Ashna Patel
Bart Stewart
Ben Ennis
Bhaskar Thyagarajan
Bhavesh Vadhani
Bilal Parviz

Brett Sortal
Brian LaFaille
Brian Foster
Bryan Prout
Catherine Roeder
Chaitra Krishna
Chandramouli (CM)
Charles Rayburn II
Charles Williams
Charlie Knowlton
Chris Halsted
Christian Conti
Diane Clarkson
Dilip Poluru
Dino Sammarco
Donna Weiss
Doug Pitek
Ed Klebanov
Emilia D'Anzica
Eric Koester
Frank Donahue
Gary Dirksen
Ginger Noce
Gul Khemani
Gunes Kulaligil
Haddis Tafari
Haniel Lynn
Hari Vittaldevara
Heather Thornton
Helen Kottenstette
Irit Eizips
Jacqueline Rockman
Jagriti Hooda
James McKenna
Jamie Dorner
Javier Caballero
Jennifer Chiang
Jeremy Hayes
Jessica Albers
Jim Lonero
Jim Luetkemeyer
John Beasley
John Downes
Jonathan Chang
Josh Sutton
Justin Catchings
Karen Cangialosi
Karen Werner
Kavitha Venkita
Kevin Tai
Kirsten Messina
Konstantin Lomidze
Krish Vitaldevara
Krishna Somu
Kristin Sherwood
Kristine French
Kyle Haran
Lauren Brennan
Lillian Bijl
Lindsey Waldrop
Madhavi Samudrala
Mark Castoe
Mark Girard
Mark Storace

Mark Tonsetic
Martin Kaufman
Michael Grant
Michael Haymaker
Michael Murphy
Miguel Donayre
Mike O'Connell
Mouhamadou Diagne
Neel Padmanabhan
Nitin Badjatia
Noel Johnson
Nora Khalili
Oris Davis
Padmaja Sastri
Pallavi Rampal
Paras Patel
Parmeshwar Bayappu
Paul Jackson
Paul Nicknig
Philip Schlemmer
Pooja Gupta
Prabhakar Goriparthi
Raj Kovuru
Rishabh Bhandari
Rob Pickering
Romona Brown
Rosa Welton
Ryan Barber
Sabriye Gill
Sachin Sampath
Sam Loveland
Sassan Saedi
Scott Fuller
Scott Wallace
Serge Terzian
Seth Belford
Shailesh Gattewar
Shounak Parida
Shourjo Dasgupta
Sonia Jolly
Stephen Michael Horning
Steve Wheatley
Surya Prakash Tenneti
Sze-Kei Jordan
Tanya Strauss
Terri Nakamura
Todd Burner
Tony Pantaleo
Umashankar Peddireddi
Venkata Uppuluri (UVL)
Venugopal Cherukupalli
Vishal Rathore

APPENDIX

INTRODUCTION

Judge, Mike, dir. 1999. *Office Space*. Los Angeles, CA: 20th Century Fox.

Schwab Klaus. "The Fourth Industrial Revolution: what it means, how to respond." World Economic Forum. January 14, 2016. https://www.weforum.org/agenda/2016/01/the-fourth-industrial-revolution-what-it-means-and-how-to-respond/.

Statista. "Total size of the public cloud software as a service (SaaS) market from 2008 to 2020" Accessed on January 16, 2021. https://www.statista.com/statistics/510333/worldwide-public-cloud-software-as-a-service/.

"The Definition of Customer Success." Customer Success Association. Accessed Jan 26, 2021. https://www.customersuccessassociation.com/library/the-definition-of-customer-success/.

CHAPTER 1

Andreessen, Marc. "Marc Andreessen on Why Software Is Eating the World," Wall Street Journal, August 19, 2011. https://www.wsj.com/articles/SB10001424053111903480904576512250915629460. Columbus, Louis. "10 Insights from Salesforce's 2018 Investor Day." Forbes. September 30, 2018. https://www.forbes.com/sites/louiscolumbus/2018/09/30/10-insights-from-salesforces-2018-investor-day/?sh=880ce636e9a3.

Customer Success Association. "The History of Customer Success - Part 1." Accessed June 16, 2021. https://www.customersuccessassociation.com/library/the-history-of-customer-success-part-1/#:~:text=He%20hired%20Marie%20Alexander%2C%20who.

Lighter Capital. "Why Do Most SaaS Startups Fail? The Startup Finance Blog." May 1, 2019. https://www.lightercapital.com/blog/why-do-most-saas-startups-fail/.

Given, Matt. "The 1 Word That Saved Salesforce from Certain Doom." Inc.com. August 15, 2017. https://www.inc.com/matt-given/the-1-word-that-saved-salesforce-from-certain-doom.html.

Skok, David. "SaaS Metrics 2.0 – a Guide to Measuring and Improving What Matters," For Entrepreneurs, January 16, 2013. https://www.forentrepreneurs.com/saas-metrics-2/.

Statista. "Total size of the public cloud software as a service (SaaS) market from 2008 to 2020" Accessed on January 16, 2021. https://www.statista.com/statistics/510333/worldwide-public-cloud-software-as-a-service/.

TSIA. "Customer Success: The Strategic, Financial and Organizational Journey by Maria Martinez, Salesforce." November 3, 2016. Video, 31:42. https://www.youtube.com/watch?v=-1FrK-WkZ9pg.

CHAPTER 2

Dhaliwal, Rav. "The Everything Department." Medium (blog) April 23, 2020. https://ravsterd.medium.com/the-everything-department-ed1aod010boe.

Bliss, Jeanne. *Chief Customer Officer 2.0: How to Build Your Customer-Driven Growth Engine.* San Francisco: Jossey-Bass, 2015.

Gainsight. "The Essential Guide to Customer Experience" Accessed June 12, 2021. https://www.gainsight.com/guides/the-essential-guide-to-customer-experience/. LinkedIn profile for Jeanne Bliss. Accessed on February 20, 2021. https://www.linkedin.com/in/jeannebliss/

CHAPTER 3

Atkins, Charles. Gupta, Shobhit. and Roche, Paul. "Introducing customer success 2.0: The new growth engine" McKinsey and company. https://www.mckinsey.com/industries/technology-media-and-telecommunications/our-insights/introducing-customer-success-2-0-the-new-growth-engine.

Kaufman, Marty. "The Roles of Success in the Customer Experience" Smartkarrot (blog) January 4, 2021. https://www.smartkarrot.com/resources/blog/best-customer-experience-role-of-customer-success/.

CHAPTER 4

Dhaliwal, Rav. "There's no such thing as post sales" Medium (blog) July 21, 2020. https://ravsterd.medium.com/theres-no-such-thing-as-post-sales-a2dd1bfb3efc.

Sellers, Amanda. "What Is the Buyer's Journey?" HubSpot (blog). Accessed on June 14, 2021. https://blog.hubspot.com/sales/what-is-the-buyers-journey.

CHAPTER 5

Almquist, Eric, John Senior, and Nicolas Bloch. "The 30 Elements of Consumer Value: A Hierarchy." Harvard Business Review. March 7, 2017. https://hbr.org/2016/09/the-elements-of-value.

Christensen, Clayton, Taddy Hall, Karen Dillon, and David Duncan. "Know Your Customers' 'Jobs to Be Done.'" Harvard Business Review. August 24, 2016. https://hbr.org/2016/09/know-your-customers-jobs-to-be-done.

Dome, Jon. "The Official Jobs-To-Be-Done Playbook." Strategyn. Accessed June 18, 2021. https://strategyn.com/jobs-to-be-done/jobs-to-be-done-playbook/#JTBD_Chapters.

Hill, Andrea F. 2019. "Confused about Jobs to Be Done? So Was I." Medium. March 1, 2019. https://afhill.medium.com/confused-about-jobs-to-be-done-so-was-i-fa2ad70672ef.

Ramdas, Shreesha. "Net Promoter Score | Is NPS Good Enough to Measure Customer Happiness? | Strikedeck." Strikedeck.com. August 7, 2018. https://strikedeck.com/is-net-promoter-score-good-enough-to-measure-customer-happiness/.

Shah, Dharmesh. "Success Is Making Those Who Believed in You Look Brilliant." Medium. June 27, 2016. https://thinkgrowth.org/success-is-making-those-who-believed-in-you-look-brilliant-446b63f99583.

CHAPTER 6

Aravindakshan, Asha. "Sprinklr's Value Realization Framework: Four Key Steps Connecting the Dots for Customers from Their Day-To-Day toward Positive Business Outcomes." Sprinklr. January 6, 2021. https://blog.sprinklr.com/inside-sprinklr-value-realization-model/. Sprinklr. https://www.sprinklr.com/ Accessed February 2021.

CHAPTER 7

Dhaliwal, Rav. "The Everything Department." Medium (blog) April 23, 2020. https://ravsterd.medium.com/the-everything-department-ed1aod010boe.

Gainsight. "How Microsoft Is Building the World's Largest Customer Success Team." April 19, 2018. 25:47 https://www.youtube.com/watch?v=L5ZzugfmmmU.

CHAPTER 8

Chiang, Jennifer. *The Startup's Guide to Customer Success: How to Champion the Customer at Your Company.* Potomac, MD. New Degree Press. 2019. Kaufman, Marty. "3 Areas That Inform Your Customer Retention Strategy." February 4, 2020. https://www.linkedin.com/pulse/3-areas-inform-your-customer-retention-strategy-marty-kaufman/.

CHAPTER 9

Gainsight. "How Microsoft Is Building the World's Largest Customer Success Team." Video, April 19, 2018. 25:47 https://www.youtube.com/watch?v=L5ZzugfmmmU.

Guedes, Angela. "Why Customer Marketing Must Live within Customer Success." Blog.nuffsaid.com. Accessed June 19, 2021. https://blog.nuffsaid.com/customer-marketing-customer-success.

TSIA. "Aligning Sales, Services, and Marketing Around Customer Success by Mark Roberge, HubSpot" May 16, 2016. Video, 37:02 https://www.youtube.com/watch?v=D8E3LvDfU8Y.

TSIA. "Integrating Sales and Customer Success in a SaaS Environment by Callan Carpenter, Autodesk" May 18, 2018. Video, 30:48. https://www.youtube.com/watch?v=mDhXlpBmpgw.

CHAPTER 10

Amar, Jorge. Berg, Jeff. Buesing, Eric. Obeid, Maurice. Raabe, Julian. "The Vision for 2025: Hyperpersonalized Care and 'Care of One' | McKinsey." June 22, 2020. https://www.mckinsey.com/business-functions/operations/our-insights/the-vision-for-2025-hyperpersonalized-care-and-care-of-one.

Cisco. "#DigitalMinds - Steve Cox" April 15, 2019. Video, 4:02. https://www.youtube.com/watch?v=mplaUeMeeto.

Customer Data Platform Institute. "CDP Basics | CDP Institute." Accessed on June 19, 2021. https://www.cdpinstitute.org/cdp-basics.

OpenView Partners. "Product-Led Growth 101: What It Is and Why It's Here to Stay." Accessed June 19, 2021. https://openviewpartners.com/product-led-growth/#.YCIDL-hKiUk.

Solomon, Karen. "How Software Subscriptions Help Cisco Earn Its Revenue | Salesforce." The 360 Blog from Salesforce. November 24, 2020. https://www.salesforce.com/blog/leading-through-change-cisco-martinez/.

Subaiya, Thimaya. "Reimagining Customer Experience: Seizing Our Opportunity Together, Today." Cisco Blogs. October 28, 2020. https://blogs.cisco.com/partner/cx-news-for-partners?_lrsc=38ec5330-aa7f-4abf-a286-d6781bac3d98&dtid=osolinoo1080.

CHAPTER 11

Cox, Steve and Subaiya, Thimaya. "Bringing Down the Silos" December 1, 2020. CX Leader Podcast hosted by Steve Walker. Podcast. 26:30. https://cxleaderpodcast.com/bringing-down-the-silos/. Sprinklr. https://www.sprinklr.com/. Accessed February 2021.

CHAPTER 12

Hagen, Paul. "The Rise of the Chief Customer Officer." Harvard Business Review. April 18, 2011. https://hbr.org/2011/04/the-rise-of-the-chief-customer.

CHAPTER 13

D'Anzica, Emilia. "How to Fix Sales & Success Friction (Hint: It's Not Having CS Report to Sales)." Blog.nuffsaid.com. November 18, 2020. https://blog.nuffsaid.com/fix-sales-and-customer-success-friction.

TSIA. "Aligning Sales, Services, and Marketing Around Customer Success by Mark Roberge, HubSpot." May 16, 2016. Video, 37:02. https://www.youtube.com/watch?v=D8E3LvDfU8Y.

CHAPTER 14

Kalra, Sachin. "The Evolution of the Customer Lifecycle." Marketo Marketing Blog - Best Practices and Thought Leadership. November 10, 2016. https://blog.marketo.com/2016/11/the-evolution-of-the-customer-lifecycle.html.

CHAPTER 15

Mehta, Nick, and Pickens, Allison. *The Customer Success Economy: Why Every Aspect of Your Business Model Needs A Paradigm Shift*. Wiley, 2020.